I0022682

Charles Fletcher Dole

The American Patriot

Charles Fletcher Dole

The American Patriot

ISBN/EAN: 9783337306533

Printed in Europe, USA, Canada, Australia, Japan

Cover: Foto ©Thomas Meinert / pixelio.de

More available books at **www.hansebooks.com**

'THE

RICAN PATRIOT

BY

CHARLES F. DOLE

AUTHOR OF

E LITTLE CITIZEN, THE CITIZEN'S CATECHISM,
TALKS ON CITIZENSHIP, ETC., ETC.

———

ISSUED BY

THE PATRIOTIC LEAGUE

ORGANIZED TO PROCLAIM THE NECES-
SITY FOR SYSTEMATIC INSTRUCTION IN CITIZEN-
SHIP IN THE SCHOOLS AND OUT OF THEM; TO CULTIVATE
THE KNOWLEDGE OF AMERICAN PRINCIPLES, LAWS, HISTORY AND
PROGRESS, AND TO INSTIL AMERICAN IDEAS INTO THE
MINDS AND HEARTS OF AMERICANS, NATIVE AND
ADOPTED, OF BOTH SEXES AND ALL AGES,
SECTS AND PARTIES

NEW YORK
THE PATRIOTIC LEAGUE

"OUR COUNTRY" SER

THE PATRIOTIC LEAGUE

THE LITTLE CITIZEN, also called " THE YOUNG CITIZEN" by F. Dole, is in the form of questions and answers, for the same purpose as the "Citizen's Catechism " but written especially for young children. Its simplicity renders it no less attractive to children of the larger growth.   **Cloth, 35 cents.**

THE CITIZEN'S CATECHISM by Charles F. Dole, revised by many eminent social and political scientists, is designed to present in compact simple form the principle ideas of citizenship. State and City School Superintendents in every part of the country have written commendations of this book, and the opinion has been expressed by several of them that ability to answer its questions intelligently should be a requisite to naturalization of foreigners. It has been adopted for use in the public schools of New York, Philadelphia, New Haven and other places.
Paper, 10 cts., cloth, 35 cts.

TALKS ON CITIZENSHIP, by Charles F. Dole follows the arrangement of topics in the " Citizen's Catechism." The two books can be used to advantage together or separately.   Cloth, 50 cts.

THE AMERICAN PATRIOT, by Charles F. Dole, discusses in the most simple and charming way the principles and right practices of citizenship.   Cloth, 50 cts.

OUTLINE OF AMERICAN GOVERNMENT, for teachers and pupils of high schools and lower grades, prepared especially for schools that adopt the Gill School City government, by Delos F. Wilcox, Ph.D. and Wilson L. Gill, LL.B.   Cloth, 50 cts.

MUNICIPAL AFFAIRS, by John R. Commons, is most instructive and entertaining about those features of the city concerning which it is the interest and duty of every man, woman and child to be familiar.   Cloth, 50 cts.

CITY PROBLEMS, by Delos F. Wilcox Ph. D., for grammar and high schools. Five chapters on Fresh Air. Light and Room for Play; The City's Waste, Life, Property and Good Order; The City's Finances; The Citizen — His Rights and Duties.   Cloth, 35 cts.

AMERICAN IDEAS, by Thomas R, Slicer, a series of talks to young people on the principles of American citizenship. In press.

WASHINGTON, abridged from Irving's Life of Washington.   Cloth. 35 cts.

FRANKLIN, by Henry M. Leipziger, Ph. D., from autobiography.   "   35 cts.

JAY, by Wm. Jay Schieffelin, abridged from Life of Jay by Wm. Jay.   "   35 cts.

COLONEL WARING, sketches by Albert Shaw and others.   "   35 cts.

STORIES FOR LITTLE CITIZENS, by Bolton Hall, John R. Commons and Miss Jennie B. Merrill, Supervisor of New York public kindergartens, and others to convey lessons in citizenship to the " wee ones,' are full of delights. This is in course of preparation.

OUR COUNTRY, monthly magazine of the Patriotic League, published at 7 East 16th St., New York, ten months each year, is $2 yearly, sample copy 10 cts. sent free to active members of the Patriotic League. The above described books are published serially, and others will follow on law, biography, history and other matters pertaining to intelligent citizenship.

THE PATRIOTIC LEAGUE is chartered to promote the cause of systematic instruction in citizenship. Membership is open to all. It furnishes to active members through OUR COUNTRY free of charge, a three years' course of instruction in citizenship. Active members pay annual dues $ 1.50, in chapters of 10 or more members, $ 1 each. Members of the Alpha Chapter pay $ 5 or more a year.

COPYRIGHT, 1899, BY THE PATRIOTIC LEAGUE

OUR COUNTRY SERIES
OF BOOKS

THIS is one of a series of small books designed by the
Patriotic League to convey some ideas of practical
patriotism and to cultivate the spirit of helpful kindness.
Such books alone, if perfectly adapted to their purpose and
put into the hands of young people, will, now and then,
prove to be good seed fallen on good ground. It is well,
however, for those who wish to be a blessing to the young
people to recognize the fact that, as a rule, putting good
books into the hands of boys and girls will not accomplish
for them the thing that each one needs. On the other
hand, they are glad to be led by older persons whom they
respect, and they must have wise and constant leading
and encouragement, if best results are to be gained.

The Patriotic League does not hope to see American
citizenship rise to the plane of perfection simply by means
of teaching the words or the thoughts contained in the
precepts of morality, but by daily and constant training
of the children in the application of right principles to
their actions at play and work, in the school and wherever
they may be. Necessary to such training is a successful
presentation of right principles, which is the aim of the
Patriotic League authors. To aid in this training and practice the President of the Patriotic League devised the
"Gill School City," which has proved to be useful for its
purpose. By this means the pupils become actual *citizens*
of a republic, instead of *subjects* of the ordinary old style
monarchical school government. In connection with this
is the "School State" and "School Republic."

The series of *"Our Country" Books* of which this book is one, is issued under the authority of the following named men and women who are officers of

THE PATRIOTIC LEAGUE

Address all mail to   P. O. Station O, N.Y.

GENERAL OFFICERS

WILSON L. GILL, Pres't,   JAMES T. WHITE, Sec'y,   ALEXANDER M. HADDEN, Treas.

COUNCIL:

ABRAM S. HEWITT, Ex-Mayor of N. Y.   O. O. HOWARD, Maj. Gen. U. S. A.
EDWARD EVERETT HALE   JAMES A. BEAVER. Ex-Gov. of Pa.
DORMAN B. EATON,   Ex U. S. Civil Service Commissioner

HONORARY AND ADVISORY BOARD:

WM. McKINLEY, President of the U. S.   JOSIAH STRONG, Pres. Social Service Lgue,
GROVER CLEVELAND, Ex-President   WM. H. P. FAUNCE, Pres. Brown University
BENJAMIN HARRISON, Ex-President   ISIDOR STRAUS, Pres. Educational Alliance
GEORGE DEWEY, Admiral, U. S. Navy   FRANCIS E. CLARK, Father of Chr. Endeav.
LEONARD WOOD. Brig. Gen. U. S. A.   W. S. RAINSFORD, D. D.
THEODORE ROOSEVELT, Governor, N.Y.   THOMAS McMILLAN, Paulist Father,
SIMON GRATZ, Ex-Pres. Phila.Bd Pub Ed.   Gen. T. J. MORGAN, Ex-Ind. Com.
C. R. WOODRUFF, Sec., Natl. Munic. Lgue   WM. A. GILES, Civic Federation, Chicago
P. V. N. MYERS, Dean Univ. of Cin'ti   MERRILL E. GATES, Ex-Pres Amherst Col
T. M. BALLIET Supt. Schools, Springfield   WALTER L. HERVY, City Exmnr N.Y. Schls
HERBERT WELSH, Pres. Natl. Indian Rights Assn.   Mrs. MARY LOWE DICKINSON
ALICE M. BIRNEY, Pres. Nat'l Congress of Mothers   JOHN LEWIS CLARK
LA SALLE A. MAYNARD,   JOHN W. HEGEMAN,   RUFORD FRANKLIN,   JACOB A. RIIS
R. FULTON CUTTING, Pres. Association for Improving the Condition of the Poor
WILLIAM L. STRONG, Ex-Mayor of N.Y., President of the Alpha Chapter,
JOHN H. C. NEVIUS, Vice Pres. Alpha Chapter,   Col. HENRY HERSCHELL ADAMS,
ARTHUR GOADBY, Sec. and Treas. "   "   ROBERT S. MacARTHUR, D. D.
WM. JAY SCHIEFFELIN, Ex-City Civil Serv. Com.   Mrs. ESTHER HERRMAN,
Gen. JOHN EATON, Ex-U.S. Com. of Edcn, late Director of Public Instruction, Porto Rico

LIFE MEMBERS:

WILLIAM E. DODGE, GEORGE D. MACKAY, WILLIAM IVES WASHBURN, BERNARD CRONSON, Mrs. JOHN L. GILL, DANIEL B. WESSON, JOHN A. CASS, HENRY B. METCALF, JOHN J. McCOOK, Mrs. SAMUEL R. PERCY, Mrs. LOUIS L. TODD.

LEAGUE INSTRUCTORS:

CHARLES F. DOLE,   THOMAS R. SLICER,
JAMES ALBERT WOODBURN, Indiana University
JOHN R. COMMONS and JAMES H.HAMILTON, Syracuse University
HENRY M. LEIPZIGER, Supervisor, Free Public Lectures, N. Y. Public Schools
M. L. DE LUCE, University of Cincinnati, KATE B. SHERWOOD,
ALBERT SHAW, Editor " Review of Reviews"
WM. C. ROBINSON, Yale College and Catholic University of America
GEORGE W. KIRCHWEY, FRANCIS M. BURDICK and FRANK J. GOODNOW,
Columbia Univ. DELOS F.WILCOX, MILO R.MALTBIE, Ed. " Municipal Affairs"

IN MEMORIAM: JOHN JAY, ELLIOT F. SHEPARD, GEO. E. WARING, JR.,
JOSEPH LAMB, SAMUEL FRANCIS SMITH.

CONTENTS

THE PRINCIPLES OF AMERICAN CITIZENSHIP
AS TAUGHT BY
THE PATRIOTIC LEAGUE

Whatsoever ye would that men should do to you, do ye even so to them.

WE BELIEVE, In the principles of the Declaration of Independence—That all men are created equal; that they are endowed by their Creator with certain inalienable rights ; that among these are life, liberty and the pursuit of happiness.

WE BELIEVE, That good character, helpful kindness, to all creatures and civic intelligence are the basis of true citizenship.

WE BELIEVE, That the public, in assuming the education of children, becomes responsible to them not only for physical, industrial, mental and moral culture, but also for special training, to the end that they shall be most happy useful and patriotic while children, and be intelligent and faithful citizens.

WE BELIEVE, That it is our duty to consecrate ourselves to the service of our country to study the history and principles of our Government, to faithfully discharge all obligations of citizenship, to improve our laws and their administration, and to do all which may fulfil the ideal of the founders of our Republic—a government of the people. for the people and by the people, of equal rights for all and special privileges for none—and to the maintenance of such a government we mutually pledge to one another our lives, our fortunes and our sacred honor.

WE BELIEVE, That we should endeavor to lead others to understand, accept and extend these principles, and to uphold and defend the institutions of our country.

THE YOUNG CITIZEN'S PLEDGE

I AM a CITIZEN of AMERICA and HEIR to all her Greatness and Renown.

As the health and happiness of my body depend upon each muscle and nerv and drop of blood doing its work in its place, so the health and happiness of my country depend upon each citizen doing his work in his place. I will not fill any post, nor pursue any business where I shall live upon my fellow-citizens without doing them useful service in return ; for I plainly see that this must bring suffering and want to some of us.

As it is cowardly for a soldier to run away from the battle, so it is cowardly for any citizen not to contribute his share to the well-being of his country. America is my own dear land ; she nourishes me, and I will love her and do my duty to her whose child, servant and civic soldier I am.

I will do nothing to desecrate her soil or pollute her air, or to degrade her children, who are my brothers and sisters. I will try to make her cities beautiful and her citizens healthy and glad so that she may be a most desirable home for her children in days to come.

I accept the Principles of the Patriotic League for my own and I will do the best I can to live and act by them every day.

THE AMERICAN PATRIOT.

CHAPTER 1

WHAT KIND OF A MAN MAKES A PATRIOT?

Men may be divided roughly into two classes. There is a very large class whose chief aim in life is to get what they can out of it for themselves. They propose to have the advantage of others. They mean to ride on top of the coach. I will not say that they deliberately intend to steal a ride. Often they do not even see that when they ride, other men are dragging them. I will not say that they are not willing to put themselves to any trouble or to exert themselves. On the contrary, they frequently show uncommon enterprise in climbing to the top of the coach and in keeping their seats. I would even grant perhaps more than Mr. Edward Bellamy, when he used this old parable of the coach, and allow that the riders imagine that it is important to all the others that they should continue to ride. They may honestly believe that the coach would not run at all unless they were on the top of it. My point simply is that a large proportion of mankind thinks it the chief object of life to ride through this world as easily and comfortably as possible. They desire this for themselves; they generally propose this for their children. We will not for the present complain that there is any harm in this. We merely state the fact that a large number of mankind belong to the class of those who wish to get for themselves all that they can. I do not know any better name for them than the selfish people.

There is also a class of men and women, who honestly
think that they are here in this world on purpose to do
their fair and full share for helping on the life of all of us.
Yes, there are a good many people who do not prefer
merely to ride through life, but if there is walking and
dragging to be done, they choose to do at least their part
of the hard work.   In short, if you could imagine all the
work of human society—all the lifting necessary for getting the world on towards the higher levels, to be divided
into units of effort, and each person in the world to be
assigned his proper portion of all this effort, while one set
of people would like to get rid of their share and to contrive to have it done for them by others, there are those
who would desire, and insist upon undertaking a little
more than their exact share of the effort.

I said that our two classes were only roughly divided
from each other.   It is hard to draw the exact line where
the sea and the ocean meet.   So there are many who
sometimes appear to be thoroughly selfish, but on occasion do quite generous and social things.   I can illustrate
what I mean in this way.   There was a man who hired
a certain farm which he proceeded to exploit.   He got off
it all that he could, and he did the least possible to enrich
it or keep the weeds down.   He let the buildings and
fences get out of repair and he cut and sold the timber.
Thus he ran the farm down so that it was nearly worth-
less to the man who should come after him.   But while
he lived by exploiting the farm, he was not altogether a
bad fellow.   He always gave a meal to the tramps who
came to his door, and he put his name down for sub-
scriptions to his church and its charitable societies.
Nevertheless, I think he belonged, on the whole, to the
class of shirks and the selfish people. So did the rich man
in the next town who made his money by a shoddy con-
tract in the war, who, however, endowed a school with
some of the money.   We shall have to put him and his
money on the selfish side of the line.

What I want now to make perfectly plain is that the selfish people have no place in a republic like ours. Other governments, indeed, have been arranged with special reference to them. A despotism, with its emperor or sultan and his parasites on one hand, and a horde of serfs on the other, was a special arrangement to allow a selfish class to exploit the others and live out of their toil and their taxes. An aristocracy of noble families was a convenient government for the same purpose. One set of people thus had the land and the offices, and the rest supported them. Nearly all Europe bore this kind of burden for centuries. Most European countries are still under it. The ancient republics too were an ingenious arrangement for selfish people to have more than their share. At old Athens, a few thousand free families lived on the labor of perhaps ten times as many slaves. When a slave became free, he wanted likewise to become a master and to lord it over others.

We have changed all this in America. As soon as anyone thought out the noble motto, "Government of the people, by the people, for the people," it was the same as putting up a notice—"Selfish people not wanted here!" Our government is founded on the great motto. It means that everyone here is to have his full share of rights, but it means also that everyone is to bear his full share of duties. Now for almost the first time in the history of the world is true human society like a great family.

If anyone gets more than his share, he gets it against the idea of a republic; he gets it as an aristocrat or a "favorite. If anyone tries to get more than his share for himself, he tries to snatch what belongs to all. If anyone, on the other hand, does more than his exact share, he makes the republic richer. If all would try to do their utmost, all would be doing what is the avowed purpose of the people of a commonwealth.

Let us put this very definitely. There is a man (we will call him Mr. Jones) who wants to be alderman in a

certain city.   Why does he want the office ?   He wants it to
please his own ambition, because he can wear a title ; or
he wants it in the hope of being mayor later ; or he
wants it for the salary, or even for the chances that it will
offer to make money.   And how does this man propose
to get the office ?   He proposes to ask all his friends to
vote for him ; he proposes to lay his wires to capture the
nomination ; in other words, as far as he can, he proposes
to elect himself.   Now what has happened to our beautiful American motto, if this man is elected?   It is government of the people still, but this is all that is left.   It is
government *by* Mr. Jones and *for* Mr. Jones.   This is the
same sort of government as they had in the time of Cæsar;
or, as they have now in Turkey.   The very idea of Republican government is gone.   The fact is, selfishness
in getting office or in using it kills the American commonwealth.

Let us take another illustration.   Mr. Smith will not go
into politics at all.   He can do better for himself.   He has
exploited a great railroad property.   He has invested
money in the Whiskey Trust.   If he were asked
to show what good he had ever contributed to the
commonwealth of America, or for what reason he
draws an income of fifty thousand dollars a year from
the labor of all the people, he could not answer a word.
On the contrary, the commonwealth is poorer than it
would be if he had never lived.   Exactly what now, has
this man done?   Under a government that exists *for* the
people, he has used the laws and the protection which
they give *against* the common good of the people and for
himself.   The robber barons who built their castles on
the Rhine to waylay those who could not protect themselves were doing nothing different in principle from
this rich Mr. Smith.   He is a survival of the evil old times.
But he is at war with the American Commonwealth; and
equally so is the clerk in an office, or the school boy who
sees this great greedy man pass, and envies him or

would do the same things, if the chance came in his way.
Call all such men and boys *foreigners* together—though
their forefathers may have come over in the Mayflower—
for they do not belong in America.   But do not call Carl
Schurz a foreigner, nor Boyle O'Reilly, nor the humblest
Russian Jew just arrived in New York, so he has come
here to add his little life to the common good and the
Commonwealth.

No man, indeed, is a foreigner here, who believes in
the motto that makes our American Government.   It
is of the people, by the people, *for* the people.

We have then at once the test of the patriot.   The
patriot in America is a different kind of man, and has a
different object in life from the Athenian
patriot, or the Florentine patriot, or
almost any other kind of patriot who
ever lived before our government was
founded. These other patriots defended
themselves and their own children; they
fought to hold their own power and the
privileges of their own class.   The American patriot lives for the great Commonwealth.   He does not defend merely
his own rights ; he does not vote for his own rights
or his own interests.   Show him what is best for all the
people.   He stands to defend and serve them.   So Washington and the founders of the Republic seem to command.   So Abraham Lincoln and the men who died in
the Civil War, urge.   What American youth will not heed
their heroic call !

QUESTIONS

Into what two classes may men be divided? To which class do you wish to belong? What harm does a shirk do?

What was the injustice in most old-world governments, as in Athens, Rome, Venice, Austria? What injustice, if any, is there to-day, when a rich man does nothing but only lives on his income?

What is the true motto of our Republic? What right has a man to wish to get a public office for his own sake? Do you know of men who are in office for the sake of the public good?

What kind of men might we call *foreigners*? Whom shall we call our true countrymen? Give your highest idea of what it is to be a patriot. Name some of our patriots and show what they did for our country. Name patriots who helped us in time of peace.

"Every man is called to the service of others."

"Not what we give, but what we share,
For the gift without the giver is bare."

Life is a mission. Every other definition of life is false and leads all who accept it astray. Religion, science, philosophy, though still at variance upon many points— all agree in this, that every existence is an aim—*Mazzini*.

Is it not when we come out of ourselves and do something for some other one; when we forget to seek after our own pleasure and seek it for another; when we are lost to our own comfort and find it for those around us— is it not then, that we are making happiest the day?

THE AMERICAN PATRIOT

CHAPTER 2

WHAT EDUCATION IS FOR

We have a new idea in America. We hold that every one must have an education. It makes no difference how poor a child's parents are. They may not be able to pay a cent for the cost of the schools. They may think that they need to keep their children at home to help them earn their bread. They may not even wish to send their children to school and the children may not care to go. Nevertheless, we say that the children of the poorest and most ignorant people in the slums of the great cities and on the plantations at the South, where the blacks live, must all have an education. We are all the time building more beautiful schoolhouses at the public expense. Some of the newer buildings are worthy to be compared with kings' palaces. We have an army of superintendents and teachers. We spend on our public education not far from one hundred and fifty millions of dollars a year. This is as though we set apart all the constant labor of 300,000 men to pay for the schools. We will not let the parents off who keep their children away from school. But in many States we have laws to require the children to go to school during a good part of each year.

I have called this plan of giving every one an education, whether he wishes it or not, a new idea in the world. Of course, there have been enlightened men, like King Alfred of England long ago, who have always believed in education. But the common idea used to be that the people who did the hard work, the slaves and serfs, did not need to be educated. Indeed, education might make the toilers discontented.

Why is it that in all civilized countries the old idea is passing away, and the new plan of educating every one is coming to be popular? Why is it that the rich people are perfectly willing to be taxed to pay for the schooling of other people's children? A great many persons think that education is "a very good thing," without knowing why. Much less, they do not know why all of us ought to be compelled to pay our share to maintain the schools, and why truant officers should hunt up reluctant boys.

ALFRED AND HIS MOTHER.

Alfred, the greatest King of early England, reigned through the last quarter of t) : ninth century. When he began to reign, there was scarcely a priest south of th.. Thames who knew the language of the people. Green, in his " History of the Englis.\ People," says that the world had never before " seen a king who lived solely for th.. good of his people." He established schools and translated books for their use.

I wish, therefore, to make it very plain precisely why w: in America believe in universal education.

Let us first, however, see what there is in some of th. reasons that people often give for getting an education. They want an education, they say, so as to be able to earn a better living and to have more money. If a man has ? good education, he need not work with his hands, he can be a clerk in a store, and rise to be a merchant, or he can be a lawyer or a doctor. A girl need not cook and wash dishes, but she can be a teacher or enter a profession. An education thus enables one "to do better for one's self."

It is in line with this same idea that we hear demands for trade schools, where boys and girls can learn carpentering and dressmaking, so that they may earn a better living. All this is very well, but what shall we do for the millions of people who must still work on the roads, and in the mines, and upon the land? We want them educated, whether they earn more money or not. We want the girls educated who cook in a myriad homes and never become teachers or doctors. We fear, if people expect education to give every one better pay, that many will be disappointed in this. The fact is, we believe in education for a better reason than the money that there is in it.

There is a generous reason why Americans believe in education. We see that many children are born into the world, with all the odds against them. They are poor; their parents do not always speak the English language; their homes are forlorn. We want to "even things up" for the unfortunate children. We want to give them a fair chance with others. We desire to open the avenues that lead up to happiness.

This is a good reason for education, but it is not the great reason. In fact, the world has found that the getting knowledge and reading books are not sure to make people happier or more capable men and women. People who read the newspapers are often the least contented. People who read may despise their own work, without being the least able to do better work.

Neither is it clear that merely sending children to schools, however excellent, really educates them. Men and women of the older generation, who had to work hard to earn their own education, were as well educated as any of us. Abraham Lincoln got a splendid education, albeit a hardly earned one. The truth is, there must be some object in education greater and higher than bettering one's own condition, whether by getting more pay, or by being able to use the public library.

The chief end of education is not sefilsh, but the public good. I will put this first in a negative way. There is a foe to our great Republic. The name of this foe is Ignorance. It began to be a foe as soon as our forefathers es-

tablished a free government.   There were always those
in the land who could not read.   It was managed for a
time that the balance of power was kept in the hands of
those who held property, who generally had education
also.   But it did not seem fair in a republic, like ours, to
keep people out of power because they were poor.   The
poor and the rich, the illiterate and the educated, were giv-
en equal power on the ground of their common manhood.
Meanwhile, a multitude of all nationalities emigrated to our
shores.   Whether wisely or not, they were speedily made
citizens.   After the Civil War, the blacks in the South
were given the ballot.

It has come to pass that at every election men vote who
know nothing of the questions which their votes help to
decide, or of the character of the men for or against whom
they vote.   Ignorant voters are led to the polls by prejudice or passion, or even by bribery.   Ignorance may easily
be made to turn an election, to the mischief of the very
men who are bribed or befooled.   Ignorance may be
cheated out of its fair vote and made to count to the credit
of oppression, or of some vile interest, such as the saloon
power.   The most selfish demagogue relies upon Ignorance to carry him to power.   In power, he relies on the
same Ignorance not to know of his mischievous practices.
Thus Ignorance is the foe of the Republic.   We must
fight this foe by intelligence.   We cannot bear to have
illiterate voters.   We cannot afford to have voters merely
read, without intelligence to ask questions about what
they read.

We want more from our schools than to fight Ignorance.
We propose to train for the public good a special class of
citizens.   We showed in the last chapter what kind of man
or woman makes a patriot.   The public schools are intended to produce patriots.   This is the great positive use of
the schools.

Let us make this point quite clear.   We can think of
certain men who have graduated from our public schools,

possibly from the high schools and state universities, and have become very successful in getting money and office. But the success of the men of whom I now speak has done vast public harm. Their money has been made at the general loss. The offices have been used, as under the Tweed ring in New York, to plunder the people. It is plain that when the schools educate men and women to help them be more mightily selfish, the schools do more harm than good.

There are also men educated at the large cost of the public, who, though they do not plunder the people or seek office for their own ends, nevertheless, are the poorest and most inefficient citizens. Sometimes they will not take the trouble to vote; or they vote as their selfish interests dictate, without asking what is good for the people. Sometimes they pay their money to help elect rogues to office, or to keep them in power. These careless citizens are no better for having an education. If the public trained only such as these, it would really be wiser not to have any public schools.

It follows that the only really good use of the schools is when they give us intelligent patriots. We need men like Peter Cooper of New York, like George William Curtis, like President Garfield. These men's education made them feel a grand sense of public duty. Their lives did not belong to themselves to do as they chose, but they belonged to the nation, exactly like that of a soldier who has enlisted and sworn to obey orders. We need a great army of such men in times of peace, as well as in times of war, who, after the words of the old Roman motto, are pledged to see to it "that the Republic receives no harm." We need such women as well as men; for whether women vote or not, all the men who are good for anything are pretty sure to come from homes where noble and patriotic women preside.

Let us fix it, then, in our minds forever, that the great end and use of the schools is to educate men and women

to be patriots. Unless the schools do this work, they are
a gigantic failure. It is because the schools are not yet
doing this great work, and also because they need all
possible help to do it better, that we believe in organizing
the Patriotic League everywhere; for the people who love
their country must join hands together in order to do anything efficiently.

I might urge upon our youth their duty to the State as
a matter of common honesty. I might show how much
it costs to give every one of them an education. The cost
comes out of the wealth of the country. The youth has
done nothing yet but receive what is given him. Whether
he is in a public or a private school he is rolling up a
debt. His honor is pledged, as soon as he can, to repay
this debt to the world.

But I will not press this matter of duty. There is something better than duty. The true-hearted youth has a
splendid privilege. There is nothing that he will ever
like better than to stand on the side of the great heroes
and patriots, and to help carry on their work. The shin-
ing examples of all the glorious past are on this side.
Justice, truth, liberty, religion are on this side. Noble
company is always on this side, as truly to-day as it was
in the time of John Milton—the company of the brave, the
faithful and the generous.

QUESTIONS

What is our American idea about education? What do the
    schools cost where you live?
What is the first reason that people give for believing in
    education? What can you say about this reason?
What generous reason is there for our public schools ?
    Do you think that education makes people happier ?
    Which is the chief reason for our public schools ? How
    is ignorance an enemy to the commonwealth?
What special kind of citizens do we aim to train? Show
    how men may be educated and yet be bad citizens.
    Give examples of the kind of good citizens that we need.
What can patriotic women do? How can the Patriotic
    League help the schools? How is it "common honesty"
    to serve the State? How is it a privilege to live the life
    of a patriot?

THE AMERICAN PATRIOT.

CHAPTER 3.

THE EDUCATION THAT MAKES PATRIOTS.

It is not every kind of education that will make good citizens, or patriots. There is a certain school of whose results I stand in fear. The school-house is excellent and quite up to the mark of the latest sanitary science. The course of study is ample and attractive. But it is whispered about among the parents of its scholars, that the master of this school worships money. His reputation is coming to be that of a selfish and shallow man. I fear, in spite of the admirable equipment of his school, that this teacher will not serve to make good citizens. Boys, like wax, will take the pattern of this kind of man. They will think it fine to be "smart" and showy. When their teacher, in his public exercises on the twenty-second of February, tells them the story of Washington, I fear a fatal lack of the thrill of genuine admiration in his voice to make the boys know the heart of a patriot. Washington held that he was in this world to serve his country. I fear that this selfish teacher will let the boys think that a man is here for what he can get for himself. So far as a teacher's influence runs this way, it is as though the arrows were not aimed at the mark. The more costly the equipment, the greater is the waste.

The first thing then that we want for the education of true American citizens is teachers of the patriotic quality. I believe that we have a great many such teachers. I

recollect one who took by storm the hearts of the boys
and girls of a certain country village.   The school-house
was little.   The scholars were not graded.   The number
of classes was too large.   There were no fine globes or
great colored maps, or any of the modern equipment in
the school.   The desks were old and hacked with jack-
knives.   But the education here went straight to the

First ··· in. Boston.

mark.   Why ?   Because the teacher knew what it was for,
and his aim was true.   He was an unselfish man, working with all his might to help the boys and girls to the
best he knew.   I would rather see a ragged Indian with
his old-fashioned bow and arrow aiming at his mark and
hitting it, than the most elegant marksman with a beautiful modern rifle, who, nevertheless, hits the wrong mark
every time.   And so I would rather have my child in the
old wooden school-house under the genuine teacher,
working to make true-hearted American citizens, than in
the great palatial city school-house without the right sort
of teacher.

The figure arises at once of one—the type of many
others—in one of these modern school-house palaces,
who is not the worse surely for the magnificent equipment with which the rich city has provided her.   No
nobler heart beats than this modest teacher's ; nowhere
will you find a more unselfish or devoted life ; no great

historic patriot ever saw more clearly the end towards
which glorious deeds move; no minister of religion in
any great city pulpit is more faithfully teaching the way of
faith, hope and love. Year by year, before each new
group of pupils, this earnest teacher, grudging no extra
time or pains, is quietly setting an object lesson of what
all education is for, namely, high-minded, unselfish service.

It must not be forgotten that, in the broadest sense, the
education of the citizen is directed from the home. What
is the ruling purpose of the home? What are the parents
thinking about, planning for, talking of? Is it the getting
the better of their neighbors or competitors? Is the current table-talk about bargains, about stocks, about corner-
lots, about parties and fashions and dress? All this is
education of a kind. It will be a rare school and mar-
velous teachers that will be able to turn the current of this
kind of home training. Who will take boys and girls
fresh from homes, where the people think that life consists in making money or in getting into society, and out
of this raw material will give us the finished product in
patriots, ready to die for the country? Yet this miracle
can be worked. Nay! It is not a miracle. For the
germ of the patriot is in every child's heart, to be found
and called into action by the touch of the first noble life
that will believe in and seek it.

Let us suppose now, what often is true, that our
scholars come from good homes, that they hear over the
breakfast table some really high-minded conversation
that their parents do generous things and steer their lives
by the stars; let us suppose that they come into the
hands of good teachers who know for what high end the
public have set them to teaching; let us try to estimate
the magnificent means which we find provided for making boys and girls into patriotic American citizens.

First, let us see what the teacher can do through the
discipline of a well graded and appointed school. A

child may come from a tenement-house in the slums, from
surroundings of filth and disorder, from slovenly rooms,
from traditions of foreign oppression and inequality. The
great school-house becomes at once the embodiment of
order, equality, justice, democracy. Promptitude and ex-
actness; kindness and obedience are required of all. From
the realm of the kindergarten upwards good-will rules.
Good-will is seen to be, what it truly is in the universe,
the sovereign authority. The sooner the child falls into
line with the regnant good-will, the better it is for him
and the happier he is. Here the child who stands out
against the prevailing order is the exception. He is doing that which hurts himself as well as the others. He
discovers disorder and misrule to be senselessness. All
the forces of the school press upon him and bind him over
to be one of the friends of order and good-will. To be
disobedient is to be a nuisance in the little world of the
school. To be selfish or unhelpful is to be isolated from
the good fellowship of his mates. To be courteous, to be
kind, to be generous is to enter into the true comrade-
ship of the school-room. Here is the citizen in the process of making. Here are traits and qualities developing,
which will make their possessor at home wherever he
carries them. Learning to be on the side of order as far
back as the kindergarten, he is not likely ever lightly to
change sides and go over to the party of disorder and mischief, when a crisis in the nation divides its friends and
its foes. He has learned to drill and keep step in the
ranks of the forces of good will.

See now what we can do with the scholar's mind in the
practice of as simple a study as arithmetic. We assume
again that the teacher knows what the arithmetic is for.
It is not merely a drill in figures. It is an exercise in
character and the handling of facts. The indomitable
figures are here always in the interest of truth and
honesty. The Almighty cannot make two and two anything more or less than four. Woe unto us if the stern

A Lesson in Cooking.

array of the figures is against what we wish or say !   But
the same figures are our friends, if we go with them and
keep on their side.   They will stand by us and defend
us.   By and by we shall go out into the world ; we shall
hold offices of responsibility ; we shall have to render ac-
counts to our fellows ; we shall have to audit the ac-
counts of other men ; we shall have to judge of the do-

Wood Carving.

ings of our public servants ; we shall have to vote on
questions of public money and credit. Will our reports be
credited? Will our opinions do good or ill? This will
depend upon the thoroughness of our arithmetic. When
we were boys and girls, did we learn to go absolutely by
the facts and the figures ?

The manual training is admirable likewise for that
which the truthful teacher educes from it. The drawing
cannot be inaccurate by a hair's breadth, without inaccurate consequences. The joints of the work must fit.

Boys' Club, Extension Class Work.

The world of law will not let off slovenly workmanship.
You cannot get into a make-believe world where the error,
the blunder, the negligence will disappear. You must
go back and correct it, or there it remains. All this is
moral and not only mechanical. The boy who has once
caught the idea will recall it, when he has to compare the
work of rogues and honest men in the fabric of the state,
when politicians and statesmen pass in review. He
who knows why a bad joint can never be made to fit,
will hardly expect a bad law to last.

Let us take now the nice work of the schools in literature and history. These studies can be made dry and
barren in the hands of a teacher who has not learned
what it is that has inspired the world's great literature
and the glorious deeds of history. Noble, disinterested,
generous and liberty-loving men and women performed
the grand deeds. The grand deeds and the noble lives
made the literature. The literature and the history appeal always to the chivalrous or heroic nature of their
readers. They call upon us also to be brave, truthful,
devoted, high-minded, enthusiastic helpers to the oppressed, friendly to all, believers in the right and the good.
We know teachers who cannot touch the great books and
the grand deeds without making sparks of sacred fire fly,
to kindle the hearts of their scholars with heroism.

QUESTIONS.

What is the test of success in good education?
What faults in a teacher would spoil the success of his
    school?
What quality do we insist upon in a teacher?
Describe the best teachers you ever knew.
What object do such teachers strive for?
What kind of bad education goes on in the homes of
    what are called "shoddy" people?
Do you think that there is something noble in every
    child's heart?
What does it mean "to steer one's life by the stars"?
What is the discipline of a school?
What is it for?

CITIZENSHIP

THE AMERICAN PATRIOT.

CHAPTER 4.

THE HAMPTON IDEA.

Before going into another class of subjects, I wish to make our idea of patriotic education perfectly plain. There happens to be going on in the Southern States of our Union a great and very interesting illustration of what we precisely mean by the making of patriots.

Among the men who served in the Civil War was a volunteer who had come to this country from the Sandwich Islands. His father, the Superintendent of Education in those Islands had grappled with the problem how to make citizens out of the native Hawaiians. The volunteer soldier rose by his intelligence and courage to the rank of a general. His name was Samuel C. Armstrong.

Before the war was over, a flash of what we call inspiration came to the young general. He saw a tremendous task that lay before our nation. It was the task of making decent and virtuous citizens out of the millions of the black race who had just been freed from slavery. They were densely ignorant; they had the bad morals of savagery and slavery; they were not used to any responsibility; they had never learned to act together like freemen; their religion was little better than superstition; and yet they were soon to be entrusted with a share in the great business of governing the nation. How could this mass of slaves be made into citizens?

Gen. Armstrong saw this gigantic task and he saw likewise the vision of a special kind of education by which the task could slowly be wrought out.

GEN. S. C. ARMSTRONG.

The great Hampton Institute near the walls of Fortress Monroe in Virginia, with its thousand students, is the memorial of this remarkable man's life. From the close of the war, putting aside all chances such as his rank, education, connections, tireless energy and rare administrative ability would have given him to amass wealth or win social and political preferment, Gen. Armstrong gave himself, heart and soul, to the humble but very grand work of helping the colored people to help themselves, and so at least to save the land from the burden of their ignorance. He began with the most modest and meager equipment and with only a few scholars.

The plan of the school was that every boy and girl in it should earn his own living. Whoever was unwilling or too lazy to pay for the food that he ate, or else to work for it, could not come to the school. There were accordingly various industries provided as fast as possible—farming and gardening, brick-making, carpentering, iron-working, dressmaking and other trades by which the few dollars a month necessary for board could be earned in hard work. Only the cost of tuition was given to those who wanted education enough to do something in order to earn it. Gen. Armstrong knew that no young person begins truly to value an education, which costs him nothing to get.

Moreover, the cardinal idea of the Hampton School was *responsibility*, or in other words, that every boy and girl owes a debt of honor for his education. The training of the school, the learning of trades, the normal department that makes teachers for hundreds of district schools—all this equipment is not provided in order that a few privileged students may learn to get their own living, to amass wealth, and to rise in the competition of life above the rest of their fellows. There is nothing selfish or personal in the aim of this kind of education. On the contrary, the whole intent is to fit boys and girls *to help and educate others in turn.* No Hampton student has been educated, or has caught the idea of his school, unless he goes out with the distinct purpose of sharing what he has got and passing it along for the benefit of his people. The vigorous self-help has a motive behind it. It is in order to help others. Just as when in the early days men got the secret of Christianity, and every one wanted to tell his friends about it and make Christians out of them, so these children of an oppressed race,

having got light and power and the secret of true manhood, want to let all their brothers and sisters into the
beautiful secret and so to give manhood to their race.

This is not merely an idea. It is actually being
worked out in bright spots all through the Southern
country. The Hampton students go to be teachers.
They are not content to receive their salary. They stir
the people to build better school-houses and to provide
school for longer terms. They start Sunday-schools and
help make a better life around them. They build decent
houses and give others an object lesson of what a true
home is. They know how to work with their own hands
and to show their neighbors how to work. They carry
skill in the trades and new ideas of better farming.
Where these students go they carry civilization, as though
a light was set up in a dark place. Where they go, other
houses are built after their model, other farms are culti-
vated with their methods, other men and women adopt
the new and better morals.

One of these Hampton boys went down into Alabama
and he started a school like Gen. Armstrong's. It has
grown to the number of more than six hundred students,
and it is a great new center for spreading the Hampton
idea.

I tell this long story because it shows what real education for America is. The black boy or girl who gets
this sort of education, with a great and noble purpose in
it to make it help others, is really getting a more thorough outfit, at less than a hundred dollars a year, than a
Yale or Harvard or Vassar student gets at perhaps a
thousand dollars a year, who yet looks upon education
as a personal privilege, as a means of making money, or
of enjoying one's self, or even like a fine dress as an orna-
ment by which to be distinguished from more common
people. Mr. Washington, the student who built up the
large Alabama school, has actually got the idea of the
broadest University Education, which many university

HAMPTON NORMAL AND AGRICULTURAL INSTITUTE.

scholars never catch at all. For this colored man sees
that he is a citizen of a divine universe ; he is working
on universal lines of justice and service ; he knows that
a man is here to add the strength of his life to make
human society more perfect and beautiful ; which un-
fortunately many very expensively educated white college
graduates do not see at all.

We happen to have a capital test of what a broad and
thorough education means. The test is, what will it
enable its possessor to do, when he is put into a new set
of circumstances. The true education fits a man "to
fall on his feet" as the saying is, wherever he is thrown.
Take away his money, send him to a strange country,
put hardships upon him, and see what he will do. Has
he any resources? Can he maintain his manly dignity
and good temper? Is he good for anything in a new
society? If not, he is not well educated, though he may
read the Bible in the orignal languages.

Now the Hampton idea of education works splendidly
in meeting this kind of trial. We can scarcely conceive
a spot in the universe, where a man who comes to contribute all that he knows for the good of others, is not
welcome. There is no place where such a one will not
be happy and at ease, or where he will not speedily fall
into his place.

The Hampton idea is truly the original design of the
first college in North America. The ancient seal of
Harvard University has the words in Latin "for Christ
and the Church." Those words meant that no one is
ever educated for one's self, but education is a great trust
and responsibility. The fact is, education is to make
leaders in the great social army. To be educated is to
become a helper and a leader for the sake of those who
are not educated. For every step of promotion upwards
a scholar takes in his school, he becomes more responsible. What will he be worth to his fellows?
What side will he take, when the issue comes between

those who menace the State and those who are trying to
save it? The colored boys and girls are getting an education to make them true Americans when these questions arise. The Hampton boy is pledged to vote not
for what he would like, but for the public good. Would
it not be a shame if the race of the white boys and girls,
who have the inheritance of the Mayflower and Bunker
Hill, had run out, and did not know any longer what they

CHURCH AND LIBRARY, HAMPTON INSTITUTE.

were in this world for; or if they were thinking of their
money and their pleasure, when the nation called for their
help, their votes and their service!

QUESTIONS.

Tell what you can of the story of Gen. Armstrong.
What was the great need in the Southern country after
    the Civil War?
What is the danger still in the South?
Why are ignorant citizens dangerous to the nation?

What does the Hampton School require of all its students?

Is it well for any one to get his education for nothing?

Will the teaching a man to earn his own living be enough to make a good citizen of him?

What sort of duty did Gen. Armstrong think that an educated person owed to others?

What is responsibility?

Is a man or woman truly educated who remains selfish?

Tell how "the Hampton idea" is spreading through the South.

Name any other schools on the Hampton plan.

How can any one be said truly to be "a citizen of the Universe?"

What ought a well educated person to be able to do, when put into new or strange circumstances?

Is there any place where a person who knows how to be useful and wishes to serve others, is not wanted?

What is the motto of the oldest college in the United States?

What does this motto really mean?

On what side is the true American always bound to stand?

What will he do, if his private interest, his pleasure, or his money is on one side, and the public good is on the other?

THE AMERICAN PATRIOT

CHAPTER 5.

OUR LIBERTIES.

We Americans take liberty as a matter of course. We forget how short a time it is since any large body of people have really been free. We do not have to go back very far in the history of our own mother-country, England, to find our forefathers subject to various kinds of oppression. The poor man could not go away from his own village to seek work, without the likelihood of being arrested and thrown into jail. No man was free to worship God as his own conscience required. If one of our ancestors had been a Baptist, or a Roman Catholic, he would have been taxed to support the Episcopal Church, and he would have been shut out from many privileged offices and honors open to other men. Till a very recent time multitudes of the English people were not permitted to vote, or to have any voice about the laws, which they were required to obey.

The larger part of our fellow men even yet have no liberty, as we in America understand it. Millions of Poles, Greeks, Armenians and others are forced to obey masters of a foreign race, and to support governments which they detest. There are still hosts of serfs and slaves in the world.

We Americans are in the habit of thinking that every-one must agree with our famous Declaration of Inde-

pendence, "that all men are created equal; that they are
endowed by their Creator, with certain inalienable rights;
that among them are life, liberty and the pursuit of happiness." The truth is, that this is rather a new idea in
the world, except with the few great thinkers. It has
been slow work, within the memory of many now living,
to disabuse the minds of Americans of the idea that black
men were not made to obey white men, and that red
men were not made for white men to exterminate.

Battle Ship OREGON.

One Means for Protecting our Liberties

Our "White Squadron" is something more than a harmless symbol of national
power and pride. It is not a flock of doves. It means Peace, only when that is con-
sistent with Justice and Honor. · · · Harsh precautions, but, unhappily, necessary
for the well-being of the Republic.—"Uncle Sam's Church."

Is it quite certain that all men are born equal? In
some ways this is not true. The children of a single
household often prove to be very unequal. So some
races of men may be more powerful, or more intelligent,
than certain other races. There are men, and there are
likewise races of men, who have uncommon qualities of
leadership. The Romans were such a race. The Anglo-
Saxons are today such a race. The government of India
is probably better under English rule, to which the Indian

people are compelled to submit, than it ever was before, or than it would be, if that people tried to govern themselves.

What then do we mean, when we repeat the words of our noble Declaration, that "all men are created equal"? We do not mean that they are all equally strong or able, but that they are all equally *men*. We mean that they are men, and not animals, or beasts of burden; and that they must be treated and respected as men.   In other words, men are brothers.   As it is outrageous for the stronger brother to impose on the weaker or younger, to get the better of him, to snatch the good things and leave the other the worst things, so it is intolerable among men to enslave or oppress the weaker ones.   As it is the part of the good elder brother to help lift the little one, where he too can see and enjoy himself, to teach him, to share the good things with him, so it is the part of the leaders of men to do their very best for their weaker brothers. Thus our American idea of equality is, that all men are to be treated on the level of their common manhood.

There is a beautiful fact of religion in all this.   When we treat men on the level of their manhood, it is because we see in them something of God or the Eternal.   The mind, the conscience, the sympathies, the humanity in men is above the range of the bodily things that we see with our eyes, and weigh, and buy and sell.   When we ask the question, how we like to be treated ourselves, or how our neighbor feels in suffering injustice or abuse, we are in a region where weights and measures and prices of merchandise do not come in.   We ask such questions as the children of God, and because we believe in one Heavenly Father of us all.   If we did not believe in God's rule of justice, if we did not see in each other anything more than the outside show of flesh and blood, we should drop down to the physical or animal standard. We know that in this animal world might makes right, and the rule of strength is justice.   In the animal world there is no law against making slaves of the weaker. It is in God's world of the mind, the conscience, and the heart, that liberty dwells.

Many misunderstand what liberty is. They think of liberty under the figure of a wild animal or a bird. Doubtless some of the immigrants who come to America, from Bohemia perhaps, or from Russia, are disappointed to find laws and to see policemen in our free country. There are children who think so. When they grow up, they propose to do as they like. Sometimes they try a little experiment of this sort when the teacher goes out of the school room. But no school would be possible, if all the scholars did all the time what each liked. Neither would human society in a city be possible, if freedom meant that all the people could do as they pleased.

What, then, is it to be free? It is not to be wild like a hawk. It is to be intelligent and to respect others. Thus, though the freest person in the United States is the President, every hour of the day is occupied by the duties which he owes to the people. The good mother in a home is free, but she has to do at almost every moment whatever will be best for her children. The teacher is free, but his freedom consists in looking after the welfare of his school. So that citizen is most free—not who does whatever he likes, regardless of the good of others—but who conducts himself for the greatest good of his fellows.

We can imagine a number of bicycle riders, each riding reckless of collision with the others; or we can suppose the riders to be careful of the rights of their companions on the road. Which set of riders will enjoy most freedom, ease, safety and swiftness of motion?

It is evident that we are far yet from being a free people. We are not free merely by virtue of having the right to the ballot, or because we can go to and fro in the land. Thus, the people of the city of New York may vote and travel abroad, but they may still be obliged to pay their money to support corrupt judges, who help to

plunder them.   Again, a man may move into South Carolina and not be free to say what he thinks about politics;
or in the same state he may have the right to vote, but if
he is a black man, he may not be able to use his vote or
to have it counted.

Neither are we quite free if there are streets in our city,
where we cannot go at night without a policeman, or if
in some parts of our country we cannot send goods without an armed guard to defend them.   Neither are we free
if we cannot safely leave our houses for a week without
risk of their being robbed.   As the bicycle rider is not
free to move in the company of reckless persons, so the
citizen is deprived of some of his liberties by the ill-will,
the injustice, the prejudices, or the recklessness of his
fellow citizens.

Moreover, a man even in free America cannot be quite
free himself, if he is very poor.   He may not be able on
account of his poverty to go and seek better conditions
elsewhere.   He may really be compelled to stay in the
city, when he would like to live in the country; his
poverty may prevent his children from availing themselves
of the free use of the schools.   Neither can an ignorant
man ever be quite free.   He will be made to do what
designing men wish, and to give them his vote.   The
ignorant man is also like the rider who does not understand how to manage his bicycle.   He not only gets in
the way of others, but his own movement is slow and
cramped, and is likely to come to grief.

The bad citizen is least of all free.   For like the naughty
boy in school, he has to be watched and policed, and
when he does injustice, he must be arrested and perhaps
shut up in prison.   If there were as many bad citizens
abroad, as there were in London two hundred years ago,
or on the Rhine in the Middle Ages, no one, good or bad,
would be free to walk the streets at night, or to travel
without weapons to defend himself.   Neither would popular government be possible, if many bad men got into

power; but some kind of a tyranny would be set up which would take away the liberties of all the people. Thus, in the old cities of Greece and Italy, the name of a republic was sometimes kept, after despots had seized the government, and deprived the people of all real rule. In truth any considerable number of greedy or unscrupulous persons, whether rich or poor, menace the liberty of all. The man or woman who wishes to live without working strikes at our freedom. The more people of that sort, the less liberty can we have.

How shall we guard our American liberties so that we may not suffer their loss, like the people in the old times? Shall we keep our freedom by an army and big guns and a great navy of fast cruisers? Or shall we prevent ignorant people from doing mischief by our courts and our jails? Forts and armies and police never kept their liberties for any people. Our only safeguard for liberty is in the intelligence and sterling character of our people.

Everyone knows how the teacher has to manage an unruly school. Such schools used to be seen in the country districts, where boys and girls had never learned discipline. They thought that they had their freedom by turning the teacher out of the school. Then if the teacher was very strong and masterful, he had to enforce discipline and strictness. He had to begin by reducing the liberties of all. The worse the school, the less could be the liberty for anyone.

On the contrary, in a university there can be almost perfect liberty for all. Where good will and intelligence are, there is liberty. So then in the state, as fast as people become friendly and faithful, as fast as they regard each other's welfare and treat each other as true men—the children of God—our liberties grow.

In the old days men used to fight for liberty. Now men who want to do something for liberty, must live the good life. Brave, generous, disinterested deeds, honest words, conscientious votes purchase the enlargement of liberty.

How long a time has any great people enjoyed liberty? What sort of restrictions to their freedom did our fore-fathers in England suffer? What nations in the world to-day have such freedom as we possess? What nations can yon mention, who are oppressed?

What does the Declaration of Independence say about men? Do men generally believe this? Do all Americans believe it? What do you think about it?

Is there any doubt about the idea, that all men are created equal? What is the truth in this idea? Is it our duty to treat all men alike? What is our duty to them as men? What is the special duty of the stronger or more intelligent?

What idea of religion is behind our thought of human liberty? In a merely animal world, is there any duty towards the weak? What constitutes real manhood?

What mistaken idea do some people in America have about freedom? What is it to be free? Illustrate who the freest persons are.

Are we in America quite free yet? Show how many of our people still lack freedom. What faults of our fellow citizens deprive us of our freedom?

How does great poverty take away a man's liberty? How does ignorance or prejudice abridge freedom? How does bad character hurt one's freedom? Why was there little freedom in the Middle Ages?

Why would it be impossible to have freedom in America, if many persons tried to get their living without doing any service in return?

How can we best guard our liberties? Why is force in-sufficient to keep out liberties? Why is there less liberty in the Republic of Mexico than in the United States? Why is the freedom less in a reform school than in a university?

What can loyal Americans do for liberty to-day? Which is the more important, to fight for liberty, or to live for liberty? Show how human liberties may be enlarged.

THE AMERICAN PATRIOT.

CHAPTER 6.

LAWS EQUAL FOR ALL.

We have seen that the American idea is, Liberty for all; not liberty such as wild beasts have, to do as they please and be eaten up by bigger beasts, but liberty to live the life of men. Another great idea in America is, *Equal laws for all.*

The Old World idea has *privilege.* This meant that a few persons, or certain classes of persons, were favorites of the Government, as in the home of wrong-headed and ignorant parents, one or two of the children will sometimes get more than their share and be treated better than the rest. If we could have visited France or Germany in the middle of the last century, we would have found a few thousand persons, rich lords and others, who were thus the parasites in the State. The laws were made for the benefit of this little minority of the nation. They had among themselves nearly all the offices and the honors and the fat salaries. They were let off easily from paying taxes such as others paid. Their children were insured places, honors and lands. These were the privileged class. They were the princes and kings and their relatives, and the groups of people who made up their courts. They made the laws themselves, and for their own benefit. Beneath them were the millions of the nation who had no voice in making the laws. They had to toil and pay heavy taxes, and work on the roads, where the rich lords rode by in their finery. The laws made them fight in the army and furnish their sons as soldiers, but they were not asked to pass an opinion whether the wars in which they poured out their blood were just or not. Thus the laws were unequal, being for the benefit of some and for the oppression of many.

I am sorry to say that in these old days one of the privileged classes were the ministers of religion. Laws were made for their special benefit. For instance, there was a privilege known as "benefit of clergy," which exempted a priest from being brought to trial in the courts like other men. The priests and bishops and monks had their own courts. Unworthy priests were thus enabled to do wrong and to escape the penalties of their crime. It came about at last that if a man who was not a priest could read, he was often given "benefit of clergy," which the multitude of unlearned men could not have. This kind of privilege was not given because the men who took it were following the principles of their religion. Jesus had never asked to be exempt from the burdens of the laws of the Roman Empire. But men took these privileges to themselves because they forgot Jesus' teachings, and fell into bad habits of making and using the laws for their own selfish ends.

The period of privilege in the Old World has scarcely yet ceased. It is only a short time since it needed either special favor or money to buy an officer's place in the British army or navy. The laws were made for the benefit of the men who had property, and especially land. They were made for those who wanted to shoot hares and foxes, but not for the poor man whose garden was ridden over by the hunter, or whose chickens the foxes devoured. The old laws are hard to change even yet. Over in Germany and in Russia, we should still find old laws and customs that make one little class of people favorites, and compel the rest to pay for privileges that are to be enjoyed only by courts, officials and kings.

The great men who brought out our American plan of government thought justice the greatest thing in the world. They were determined to have no favorites here, and no class of men who should enjoy privileges that other men must pay for. They would not let any American set up a title of nobility, as though he and his family were made of different clay from the rest of us. Washington, Franklin, Jefferson, Adams, and their friends,

The French Castle Chateau du Moutier.

"PRIVILEGES THAT OTHER MEN MUST PAY FOR."

the ablest, the most intelligent, the most prosperous men of their time, held that the same laws which were best for the people, were best also for them. They scorned to ask any privileges for themselves.

It is hard for us to-day to realize what a great step in advance this idea of Equal laws for all, was. We have all become used to it, and accept it like an axiom in

geometry.   The officers of the government do not plan,
as officers of the government once planned and plotted,
to hand down their offices to their own sons, and to
make their salaries hereditary.   The men in Congress
and the Legislatures do not dream that they have any
right to frame laws for one class of the people and not
for all.   The ministers of religion, to-day, do not ask the
government to grant special privileges for their sake.
What is good for the others is good, they think, for them.

A great and beautiful thing follows from our American
idea of equal laws.   It appears that our way is vastly
better, not only for the great multitude of the people, but
it is better also for the rich, and for the government officials, and for the educated, and for the ministers of
religion.   We know what happens in the body whenever
there is a rush of blood to the head or to the stomach.
The extremities are cold and fail to be nourished, and in-
flammation sets in, perhaps, to the destruction of the
brain or the stomach, where the excess of blood is con-
gested.   What is needed for the thorough health of the
body is even and regular circulation of the blood.   Every
part must be fed and warmed ; each little cell and tissue
must have its share.   And when the whole body is not
thus equally supplied, the great central organs soon
suffer.

It is so in human society and in the State ; it is so in
the family.   It is not only not good and fair to the others
to treat a few with favoritism ; it is very dangerous to
the favorites.   It was dangerous to Joseph in the old
Bible story, that his father treated him better than the
others.   This tempted him to be conceited and to tell his
dreams to his father and mother, and it tempted the
other brothers to hate him.   It was dangerous in old
France to be a nobleman and to have privileges.   Men
and women became vain, idle and selfish.   The nobleman's children were spoiled.   The poor, who had to pay
the taxes in order to support the grand court, came to

hate the privileged people. The terrible Revolution came and the unjust laws were swept away in a river of blood.

On the other hand our equal laws serve to keep the body politic healthy and well nourished. Our laws aim to give justice to the poor on even terms with the rich. Our courts are open to all alike. The laws provide that all shall be taxed on the same scale. If the laws wish to spread prosperity among all, the whole land is richer and all are the more contented. If all could be well fed, comfortable and happy, the leaders of the people, the richer people, the better educated, the ministers of religion, the government officers and the legislators would then be really succeeding in accomplishing the ends for which leaders exist. As when the officers of an army see to it that all their men are well provided for, clothed, equipped and fed, it is so much the better for the officers and the staff, who are the more likely to lead the army to victory. Whereas, a Chinese army in which the officers look out for themselves and let the soldiers starve, at last brings officers and all to ruin.

I have said that our laws aim to be equal for all. This is our American theory. I have not said that we have quite succeeded in getting equal laws. The fact is, when for many centuries things have been wrong, it is not easy at once to make them right by our votes. The habit of privilege or of unequal laws is like a chronic disease — rheumatism, for instance. The man still limps after you begin to cure him. So the old customs and laws that were made by property holders for themselves, are not got out of the minds of our Anglo-Saxon race simply because our fathers have written the words of our noble Constitution and our Bill of Rights. We fear that selfish men still often go on trying after the old way to use the laws and the courts, and even to contrive to pass new laws for the interest of their own business, for their own special protection, for their own party or sec-

tion.   We have heard of laws even in America that were
not framed for the good of all the people.   We have
heard of taxes that seemed not to bear very fairly on the
shoulders of all.   Nevertheless we have learned the
American idea.   If men ever use the laws wrongly, or
slightingly, or as partisans, for the sake of the North,
the South, the East, or the West, we know that this is a
kind of treason to our common flag.   If our legislators
ever do these things, we know that they ought not to
stay in the Legislature any longer.   We will call them
home and send men who will serve the people, and the
whole people.

QUESTIONS.

What is our American idea about liberty ?   What is our
   idea about the laws ?

What was the Old World idea in making laws ?   What
   sort of favoritism prevailed in France or Germany ?

Illustrate how this favoritism worked.   Who bore its
   burdens ?

What was " benefit of clergy " ?   What do you think that
   Jesus would have said about this ?   Show in what
   ways the period of " privilege " still lasts.

Who were the men who made our American government ?   What did they aim to effect ?   Why is it
   wrong to get privileges for one's self that the laws do
not give to all ?

What harm do unequal laws do to the few who seem to
   profit by them ?   How does French history illustrate
   this ?   How do our equal laws really serve the rich
   better than laws specially made for their benefit ?

Show any respects wherein we have not made our laws
   equal for all ?

What remedy have we, if our legislators make selfish, or
   sectional, or partisan laws ?

THE AMERICAN PATRIOT

CHAPTER 7.

RIGHTS AND DUTIES

The Americans, as we have seen, are a good people for getting their rights.   They do not propose to let anyone have honors, powers or privileges which all the rest cannot have also on equal terms.   They are accustomed to tell the children in their common schools that the highest offices in the land, the governorship, the supreme court and the presidency, are within the reach of the sons of the poorest. Whereas, in the old times, a very few men were entitled to be called lords or masters, and even in the earlier days of our own country only the wealthy or better educated were allowed to use a title, it has become a custom now to prefix the sign "Mr.," the abbreviation of "master," before the name of the humblest citizen of the republic, and the corresponding title of "Mrs.," or "Mistress," before the name of his wife. This democratic custom stands for the fact, that in America every man thinks that he has rights equal to every other man.   The equal laws are intended to secure him in these equal rights.

There is another side to all this urgent insistence about our rights.   If it is a good American idea that we are all bound to get our rights, it ought to be an equally good American idea that we all have our duties too.   This is the reverse side of the same shield.   We may express it in this way, namely, that every right carries with it a corresponding duty.

The fact is, there are two opposite ways of getting our rights in this world. One way is by force, as when the strong man helps himself to whatever he thinks is his — yes, and very often helps himself to what belongs to the others. The other way to get rights is by helping one another. This is true human society. It means that everyone gets his own rights by seeing to it that the others have their rights. For how can anyone in the crowd of men get what is his due unless all with one

The Way that was found necessary in 1776 for obtaining our Rights
A more humane Way is by extending the Principles of the Patriotic League

consent help one another. This is what the great Chinese teacher, Confucius, called *reciprocity*. It is what Jesus meant when he gave us the Golden Rule. You want your rights: "Very well!" Jesus says, See then that your neighbors get their rights. Your rights are the others' duties; your duties are the others' rights. The right on either side translates into a duty on the other side. Whoever wants his own rights without being willing to do his corresponding duties in return, has the spirit of the thief. He wants to have the use of the laws, but he does not wish to keep them himself.

All this is very hard for many persons to learn. The

truth is, that they are greedy about their rights; they can scarcely see how they will get their rights unless they assert them and claim them.   They are unwilling to trust that if they do their part and look out for the rights of others, in other words, attend to their duties, others will give them their rights.   They remind us of children who have been brought up with bad table manners.   They have been accustomed to help themselves and to hurry and snatch in fear lest the others shall get more than their share.   When these children first see a decent and civilized table where everyone waits his turn and each is quick to serve the other, they do not know how to behave.   Nevertheless this is the only kind of table where everyone is sure to be supplied.   So, precisely, in our democratic form of government; if we want our rights the only way to get them is to see, as we do at the table, that everyone else is served too.   In other words, in our free and equal American government, for the very reason that we insist upon larger private rights for each individual, we have to say more about public duties and public spirit than anywhere else in the world.

I have said that every right carries with it a duty.   Let me illustrate how this is so.   Here the freeman has a right to vote equally with every man.   But when this has been said, only a half, and that the less important half is said.   To vote is not so much a right as a duty. We vote not merely in order to get and to defend our own, but also that we may each see to it, in the language of the old Roman orator, "that the republic suffer no harm."

So also I have a right to the use of the streets, the police, the courts, the fire department, the parks and the public library.   Suppose now that I had my rights, and even more, that I was able by my influence to procure at the public expense a sidewalk and a street lamp before my fellow-citizens generally could enjoy these privileges. Suppose that I was sure of justice, while others, poorer than I was, did not always obtain justice; could I be content with getting my rights? On the contrary, I am responsible for the mischief, if any of my neighbors fail of their full right also. Whatever I enjoy at the public expense I am bound to help the others to enjoy.

Or, take the case of the public offices. I have a right to be eligible to office, but this is only half of the truth. I have also a duty if the State needs me to serve in an office. I must be able to show good reason for declining to serve. But perhaps I want office. I have a right, I claim, to the office, its honors and its salary. There is, however, a more important question. The question is, whether it is my duty to seek the office. It may be my duty to decline it. The office is not for me, but for the sake of the public. I have, therefore, really no right or claim to an office unless I am fitted for it, and unless I take it to serve the State.

I have touched, merely for the purpose of illustration, upon very important subjects, which demand fuller explanation elsewhere. My point here merely is to urge that there is nowhere a right which does not prove, when turned around, to have a duty on the other side of it.

There is a profound reason why this is so. We live in a universe. This means that everything is bound up in close ties with everything else, and every person with all other persons. In a strict sense we are all "relations." In the outward world you cannot strip the forests from the hills and not hurt the farmers and the millers who live beyond the hills. So in the world of men, you cannot build up or burn down a single village without affecting also the nation for good or evil. If in the South, or on the frontier, or in the city of New York, there are men who go without their rights, it is as though there were disease or a sore place in the body. That sore place must be cured or the whole body will suffer. For each little cell in the body is not there merely to exist, to thrive and to draw sustenance for itself; it exists and has its right to be nourished for what it is worth to its neighbors and to the whole body also.

This is not all. We do not live merely in a universe. It is a growing universe. Old things, outworn customs, inadequate laws, all pass away and give place in each age to better customs, more just laws, more free institutions. If this is so, men have to grow better likewise. The world has no use for the kind of savage men who once flourished by the rule of force. Thus our American Indian must become civilized or else disappear; the world is becoming tired of the men who crowd around the table of life, snatching the good things each for himself. Such men have had their day in the growing universe, which sloughs off the things which it outgrows. The world now asks for a higher order of men. America, at least, must have this higher life in order to match her higher institutions, her equal laws and her liberties. Enough has already been said by men who demand their rights. The city, the state and the nation now ask for men who will talk about their duties and insist upon doing their duties. The idea might once have been, "Our rights first, and let other men do their duties." The new idea is, "Our duties first, and our rights will come the more surely."

The learned men tell us that the earth, ages ago, was tenanted with immense, ugly, awkward, stupid creatures that lived in the slime. But at last in the process of time the mammals appeared, superior, with better brains, smaller perhaps, but more powerful, and the great saurians disappeared. The world had no more use for them except as specimens in a museum. And then later, man came and the day passed away for all noxious beasts. More and more the animals must serve and help man or vanish before him. The gentle ox, the intelligent horse, the friendly dog, the useful sheep, the beautiful birds of the air, might remain; but the days of the bear, the wolf and the tiger were numbered; only the higher and helpful thing could stay. The creature which tried to live for

itself alone was not wanted any longer in the growing
and divine universe.

So it is with the different orders and types of men. The
injurious, the grasping, the selfish have their day like the
ancient creatures of the slime. The new age is already here.
The new call which America is making is for the men and
women who are here for their duties, not for their own
rights alone, but that all may have equal rights.

QUESTIONS

What is it that Americans are urged to get? Show how
this is.

What is the reverse side to the subject of "rights?" What
was the old way of getting rights? What better way
is there to get our rights? What famous Chinaman
taught this idea? What did Jesus teach about it?
Why do many persons fail to understand Jesus' idea?
Show the advantage of good table manners over bad
manners. What is the idea of the civilized table manners? In what kind of government do people get their
rights most fully? In what kind of government do we
have to say most about the duties of the people?

Show how the right of voting carries a duty with it.
What is the right of voting for?

What duty does the more influential citizen who can get
his rights owe to his humbler fellow-citizens?

Would you call office-holding a right or a duty? Has
any one a right to an office which he is not well-fitted
to fill? If not, why?

What does it mean when we say that we live in a
"universe"? Illustrate how we are all related.

Show how harm comes to all of us when even a few
persons fail of their rights. What are the little cells in
the body for?

What do we mean by saying that the world grows?
What becomes of the things that the world has outgrown? Why must our Indians become civilized if
they wish to live? Is this fair?

What order of men do our American institutions demand?
What idea matches with our institutions?

Tell about the ancient creatures of the slime. What kind
of animals are now permitted to remain? What kind
of men are like the ancient creatures?

CITIZENSHIP

THE AMERICAN PATRIOT

CHAPTER 8.

THE BUSINESS OF RULERS

Our American system of government makes all the people rulers.* For the sake of convenience they delegate their power to those whom they choose to serve them as representatives and other officers. Queen Victoria or the Emperor of Germany may have ministers or governors who shall hold and use the royal authority. But as the Emperor also takes back the power that he has delegated and names other governors or generals, so the people in the United States at every election take back their power into their own hands and make fresh appointments. Their President and Representatives may carry out the wisest policy that they can devise and may make laws for the time, but the people always hold the power to change the policy of the government and to require their representatives to make new and different laws. It is the people, therefore, who are the rulers, while the officers of government are the ministers of the people.

This is a very remarkable experiment. The world has not yet ceased to wonder how it can be possible to make all the people rulers. Doubters still shake their heads and say that our experiment will not work. They tell

* In most of our States the suffrage is limited to the men. But this limitation is obviously the survival of an Old-World custom in the treatment of women. It is not in line with the general ideas of government in America, and there are many indications of coming change in this direction of the removal of the arbitrary barrier which has shut out women from full citizenship.

us that we have so far only begun to try it. "In the main," they say, "your government has really been carried on by the wiser few, by those who own property, who have succeeded in keeping the power and in framing the laws. The people have generally allowed the few to manage for them. But when the many have become the rulers, as in New York City, see how near they have come to wrecking the government! Wait till the multitude take the power into their own hands and make the laws themselves, and see what will become of your American institutions."

There are many answers to this gloomy prophecy of those who do not believe in the people, but it is no use to deny that there is actual danger in this direction. Other governments have broken down. History is the story about their rise and fall. Who shall secure us that our own government can stand firm through the thousands of coming years? Indeed it is largely our faith in human progress, which is another name for our faith in God, that enables us to believe that we have got a secret, such as earlier men did not possess, for keeping our government.

We have already agreed that we have got a new idea of patriotism in America. The patriot with us is not the man who will fight for his king or his class or his own home, but he stands for the rights of all classes and to defend all homes, even of his poorest brothers.* We have agreed also that a good citizen has something more to do than to look after his own rights. He has duties along with his rights, and the only effective way to get his rights is to do his duties, which are his neighbors' rights.

All this becomes even clearer as soon as a man, in addition to being a mere citizen, takes the office of a ruler. The first business of a ruler is to look after the interests of the whole Country. He is a ruler for the

---

* Of course the very best and noblest men in former days had this idea of the patriot. We mean this; this idea is now coming to be popular.

sake of the millions of others. This was seen by the men of the old times. When the ruler was the man, the king, they judged him a good or a bad king, according as he watched and defended the interests of his people.

The story is told that when the great Charlemagne saw the fleet of the piratical Northmen off his coasts, he wept in sorrow for the days to come when he could no longer beat the pirates off. The famous Emperor Marcus Aurelius had lived altogether for his empire. He had shortened his own life in the camps by the side of the Danube. Even ambitious and tyrannical rulers, Alexander, Cæsar, Napoleon, had to pretend, and perhaps even believed themselves, that they were fighting for their people, for Greece, for Rome, for France.

The same was true when in old England the government was really in the hands of a little group of great noblemen, the Whig lords. These men had to persuade themselves that they were ruling for the sake of England. They knew that they had no semblance of right to be spending the money and the blood of the people for themselves. For everywhere the world has long ago found out that a ruler's whole business is the welfare of the people. And when a ruler, like the terrible Borgias in Italy, or the Sultan in Turkey to-day, rules for himself, he is a despot and a traitor.

Now this principle is just as true when the rulers are many as when there was only one. It holds good for every citizen-king of the United States as for the Emperor William. The Emperor William would be a bad ruler and a traitor to his people, when in any question that arose concerning the welfare of his people, he decided for his own selfish pleasure or his pride, and against the people; so when a question concerns the welfare of the American people, and any of them chooses merely for himself and lets the welfare of the people suffer, this citizen-ruler is as bad as the selfish, stubborn or proud king, who misuses his power.

Let us make this point very clear. From time to time the millions of our American rulers have to choose what the policy of the government shall be in the difficult questions of Free Trade or Protection. I have nothing to say here as to the respective merits of these opposite sides. What I have to say is, that it is the business of the rulers to look out for the welfare of the whole people. The question for a bad ruler might indeed seem to be, "Which side shall be for my own interest?" But the question for a good ruler is, "What will most benefit the Country?" And what will benefit it, not only for to-day, but for the future also. We have all admitted that a man ought to ask this as a patriot, and as a ruler this is a man's chief business to ask.

Suppose now that some man thinks that the policy of a high tariff will help him to make money, and he never takes any pains to find out what will be the effect of this policy upon the people in other kinds of business or upon the farmers. Or suppose that a man on the other side merely hopes that the policy of Free Trade will help him buy his coats and his books cheaper, and he does not care what happens to manufacturers or miners; men, in their way, are doing the same sort of thing which our forefathers beheaded King Charles for doing. King Charles used the power to get his own selfish will; and that is substantially what selfish rulers are always trying to do.

I make this point about the bounden duty of our citizen rulers more emphatic because many persons do not recognize it at all. They know that it is true for a monarchy, but they have not opened their eyes to see that it is true in a republic. They seem to think that the duty of a citizen-ruler is only to choose whatever seems to be for his own interest. They imagine that what is good for all of us will thus grow out of a conflict of all sorts of opposing selfishnesses. With these persons the position of the ruler in a republic is a sort of a tug-of-war team, where each side pulls as hard as it can against the opposite side.

One might as well say that jurors, when they decide a case of justice, were chosen to pull against each other in a self-willed tug-of-war.   As the jurors sit for justice, so the ruler in every case is, as it were, under oath to regard the general welfare.   What should we think of a group of citizens who, if they became sufficiently numerous, used their power to get places and offices for themselves, or to tax the rest of the people for their own benefit! But this is what every citizen-ruler is willing to do who chooses the policy of the government with an eye merely to his own advantage.

All this is clearer yet when we make one of our citizen-rulers a delegate in behalf of the rest in the city Council, the Legislature, the Congress, or in any other office. Now he becomes doubly responsible.   He is ruler in his own right, and as such bound in honor to act for the good of all, and he is also specially chosen to act for others.   He is doubly a traitor too if he is planning to get something for himself by the use of his power.   The one thing that he sits in office for is the good of the people.   What shall we think of him if he sits there in order to benefit his own business or to make money faster than other men, or to distribute offices to his relations!   This man is either very bad or he has not got the kindergarten ideas of an American citizen.

But some one asks, "Is not the man in office to help his party?"   What is his party for, we reply.   Is it for plunder or for the few and not for the many?   What right has a man to belong to any party which is not seeking the interests of the people?

One thing more; it is an ancient truth, that in order to learn how to rule we must first learn how to obey.   This was in the famous motto of the Black Prince, "Ich dien," *I serve*.   This has been the thought of the great and good rulers.   There was not one of them who was merely a ruler to command. They obeyed while they ruled. They obeyed the laws themselves and therefore they enforced them. They obeyed the voice of justice, which is the voice of God in their own hearts. They obeyed the promptings of their humanity. This is our American idea for our millions of citizen-rulers. They are good for nothing to rule unless they obey. Show them what is right and they will pour out treasure and life to fulfill it. If our people get this thought, our Country can never perish.

QUESTIONS

Who are the rulers in America? Show how their representatives get their power.

Why do we call the American idea an "experiment"? What do some say in opposition to it? Why do you think that our experiment will succeed?

What did we agree in Chapter 1. as to the American idea of a patriot? What have we agreed was the way to get our rights?

What is the main business of a king? Give instances of good kings. What is the real business of the rulers in an aristocracy? What do we call rulers who only rule for themselves? Do we change the principle when we in America make all the citizens rulers? Illustrate what the citizen-ruler is for in deciding the policy of the government.

What mistaken idea do many persons still have about our rulers in America?

What double responsibility rests upon our Representatives and other officers? What are they in office for?

Is a man in office to help his party? What is the only use of a party?

What was the motto of the Black Prince? What does the motto mean? Show how great rulers have had to obey. What idea will make our Country secure?

CHAPTER 9.

WHO THE PRIVILEGED CLASS IS IN AMERICA

We have seen that there were "privileged" people in the old world. They were those who owned great tracts of land; or whose fathers had been princes, or the friends of kings, or mighty soldiers. Such as these, having inherited wealth or a noble name, enjoyed privileges apart from other men. Thus, in Germany, the army officers have had to be "gentlemen," that is, men of "good families," and not the sons of the peasantry or the poor. The privileged class have held themselves to be of finer clay than other people. They have often fenced themselves about so as not to let the "lower classes" enter their charmed circle. They have tried to forbid their sons and daughters from marriage out of their own rank.

It must frankly be admitted that there are differences of power and position in America. There are some differences which ought not to be. There are families who think themselves better than others merely on account of their name, or of some illustrious grandfather. There are those who imagine that the mere fact of having money raises them into a kind of noble rank. We have not kept all the snobs on the opposite side of the Atlantic.

There is a dangerous kind of privilege which we have let some unprincipled persons get for themselves, when we have suffered selfish men to manage politics, to name themselves or their friends for office, and thus to control our government for their own ends.   This has been a sort of privilege like that of the old world, which one man enjoys and others have to pay for.   When a Senator or a Representative in Congress has thought himself to have the right to fill certain offices in his State or district, this was exactly the same as when a nobleman of France or England in the old times exercised the privilege of drawing pay or pensions for his own relatives from the treasury of the realm.

There are, however, real and honest privileges which some men may enjoy and others may not deserve. There are such privileges in a school when the older and more intelligent scholars may have a freedom, for instance, of communication with one another, of going to the library for books, or of discussing with the teacher in the class room, such as could not be permitted to young pupils.   It is indeed true, as we have seen, that the laws of the state must be the same for all.   But there are actual differences between men in a republic as truly as in a monarchy.   The common laws do not level away these differences.   There are therefore natural differences in the power, the influence and the position which men reach.   There are those who have distinct advantages even in America, and they make our privileged class. Let us see what constitutes "privilege" with us, and let us discover whether there is not a good meaning in the word.

In the first place, skill of any sort gives advantage or privilege to its possessor.   This has always been true in some degree, but in the old world the man of skill, if he happened to be poor, was sadly cramped in the natural enjoyment of his skill.   He might be a slave; then all his earnings would be taken away from him.   The man of skill must give way to the man of the sword.   In America we have changed this.   The abolition of slavery lifted the last curse that had once been put upon labor.

More and more the demand is for skilled men. The great corporations cannot find enough of them. The land is full of stories of the rise of such men from poverty to high positions. Edison is only one of a growing number of honorable names of our privileged class of the skilful.

A thorough education also confers natural privileges. It may or may not be a college education. It may be the education of the " University of the World," through the costly discipline of experience. We mean the sort of education that fits the mind to do any task, or to fill any position to which it may be assigned. We mean the power of careful, honest, sustained thought. We mean if any question arises, public or private, the precious habit of candor, fairness, deliberation, freedom from prejudice. Here, for example, is the question about the Monroe Doctrine and the duty of the United States concerning the governments of South America. It is education that counts, whether in the White House or in Congress, or in ten thousand newspaper offices through the Country. Half educated men may make speeches and write articles and indeed stir up a great noise. But the men and women of real education have the advantage in the long run. What intelligence, justice and sound sense determine must come to prevail.

The frugal and virtuous are also a privileged class in America. There have been times when everything seemed to be against the plain and frugal people. The king taxed them; the nobles lorded it over them; the soldiers plundered them. There are parts of Turkey now where the frugal and virtuous seem to be at a disadvantage by the side of robbers. There may be exceptional cases in the factory towns or the mining camps of our Country, where the virtuous poor have to suffer. But the rule in the United States is altogether the other way. The rule is, that the frugal, industrious, honest, temperate families are rising from the ranks. They come from

Canada, Ireland, Italy, Germany. They are trusted everywhere. They pay as they go; they do not run into debt; they begin to save. Presently they own houses, shops or farms. They send their children to school; it may be to college. They found families. In other words, the family tree, rooted in thrift and virtue, grows tall and fine. There is no more respectable tree in America, so long as it grows out of the old stalwart root of virtue. Tell any employer or any constituency, that a man has come of one of these thrifty, honest families, and you have established a prestige for his success.

It also begins to be discovered that friendliness, or good temper, constitutes privilege. The old idea of a lord or a king was of a fierce, arrogant, insolent man. We do not want such men in America anywhere. We do not even want them as soldiers or policemen. Give us men who are kindly, courteous and obliging. Give us men who like to do favors, who are considerate of others' feelings. We want such men as our overseers in 'factories, superintendents on railroads, and directors of corporations. We are finding that these are the only kind of employers or officers who are decent or fit to handle forces of men, or to carry on public business. The friendly men are thus coming to be privileged men. They are the coming race !

I have already hinted wherein " privilege " in America consists. It is not in being let off from what others have to do or pay. It is not in having honors or places which one's grandfather has handed down. It is the fair and just privilege of power, influence and leadership. It is the privilege of serving the public, it may be without pay, more than others are able to serve. My rich neighbor has risen by his simple skill from a poor boy. He throws but one vote. But his influence in the town is worth a hundred votes. He never went to college, but people believe in his good judgment, and when he rises to speak, everyone listens and goes home to think about what he said. What is more, they believe in his manliness and sincerity. He says exactly what he thinks. They know that he is public-spirited and that he will give his money along with his influence to benefit the city. They may or may not ever send him to Congress. But this neighbor of mine is a privileged character in the city. He counts for a thousand such men as I see hanging around the doors of the saloons. Yes, he would count for hundreds of some rich men, such as I know, foolish, idle fellows, if he had no wealth, but was only plain John Smith, so long as he kept his skill, his intelligence, his integrity and his large-hearted friendliness.

There is one favorite American idea that needs to be stated about our privileged class. We hold that there ought to be freedom of opportunity to get into this class. The trouble with the old-fashioned kind of "gentlemen" was, that they did not care to have all the boys become gentlemen like themselves. They meant to have a class beneath them. We say the opposite in America. We aim to give every boy and girl a good clear chance to get up into the rank of our ladies and gentlemen. Our rank includes all those who have the feelings of true ladies and gentlemen. It is based on skill, intelligence, character and a kind heart. We do not think that the way is yet open for all our millions of children in America into this higher rank. There are children whose homes are not good enough to give them an even chance with others. There are parents whose wages are not sufficient to allow their children the splendid opportunities of our public schools. There are too many saloons where ignorant people waste their earnings, and their children suffer. Nevertheless the great American idea grows: *Give every child his fair chance!*

QUESTIONS

What is "privilege"? Who were the privileged people in the old world? Is there such a thing as "finer

clay " in human nature ?   Are there real differences
between men ? If so, what kind of differences are
there ? Ought a man to be respected for his family
name ? Give reasons.   What bad privileges exist in
America ?

Give examples of skilful men or women and of what
they have accomplished.   What advantage have such
men in America ?

What is your idea of a thorough education ?   What will
it do for anyone ?   Do you think that educated men
and women get credit for as much as they deserve ?

What is property ?   Is it always possible for frugal and
industrious people to " get ahead " in America ? What
is the general rule ?   Can you give instances to illustrate your answer ?   What faults prevent great numbers of people from getting any influence ?

What has friendliness to do with getting on in the
world ? Is it a good reason for being friendly, that you
will get on better so ?   What better reason can you
give ?

What is the difference between old world privilege and
such privilege as we allow in America ?   Show how it
is a privilege to be able to save and help others.   What
privilege did Gen. Grant or Lincoln enjoy ?

How can one man often " count " for more than others ?
Who counts for the most ?   Who counts for the least ?

What favorite idea have we in America about an equal
opportunity for all ?   Where do children fail of a fair
chance ?   What do we need to do to set all the children right ?   What is the highest idea of a gentleman
and a lady ?

Lenity will operate with greater force, in some instances, than rigor.   It is, therefore, my first wish, to have
my whole conduct distinguished by it.— *Washington.*

CITIZENSHIP

THE AMERICAN PATRIOT

CHAPTER 10.

THE MAJORITY

WE SAY in America that the people rule, or that the people are the kings. There was one glorious moment in our history when this seemed a simple thing. It was immediately after we had agreed to accept the new Constitution, and all the young Nation, with one consent, wished George Washington to be their President. But our people at once began to divide into parties, and after Washington's time they could never agree again to desire any one man as their President. Even in a town it is a rare event when all the people want the same mayor or Board of Selectmen. In fact, hardly any subject can be proposed to the people against which some have not objections. What shall we do when we have millions of voters and they will not agree?

In the old times, for instance among a tribe of savages, they would often settle such a difficulty by fighting. Thus might made right. Long before men were civilized, however, they had learned to "count heads," or to vote, and they found that this was a better way for settling their differences of opinion than to fight. In America, the appeal to the ballot is the one, great, established way by which we do all the political business of the Nation. We have made it a sort of motto of our Government — *The majority shall rule.* The Civil War made that motto more solid than ever. For when a part of the Nation

brought upon us the old, barbarous "trial by battle," and
thousands of millions of money were destroyed, and
hundreds of thousands of lives were sacrificed, it was
burned into our National memory forever, we trust,
that we must settle our differences like civilized men by
our arguments and our votes, and not like savages, by
killing each other.

Is it not a rude way, however, to count hands or
heads, and then to let the majority rule ?   Suppose that
the majority of the voters are ignorant, while the more
intelligent people are on the other side.   Suppose we
lived in Mexico, and the vast majority of the people could
not even read their votes.   Suppose the majority are in
the wrong.   Suppose that they are in favor of an unjust
institution like slavery, or that they wish to engage the
whole nation in a shameful war.   Suppose in the town,
that the majority favor the liquor business and will not
even restrict it; or that they propose to levy taxes upon
all the people for hurtful expenditures; or that they will
not vote to support good schools.   Is it fair that a majority shall rule when that majority is not worthy of the
power ?   By what rule of justice must the majority rule
in such cases as these ?

It must be owned that our standard American motto is
a rude method after all.   It is better and more humane
than fighting, but it often resembles fighting, in so far as
mere numbers, as in an army, are set over against other
numbers.   To show that a larger number of citizens
desire a certain man for President surely does not prove
him to be a fit man for that high office.   To show that a
majority of men prefer a tariff does not prove anything as
to the wisdom or justice of a tariff.   In fact, it has frequently happened that the vast majority of men at a
given time have been wrong, and only a few individuals
have been right.   How would Socrates or Jesus have
been put to death, if majorities could be trusted ?   A
strong case could be made from human history, that

with regard to all reforms and changes of custom the majorities have always begun by being in the wrong.

It seems therefore, at first, as if we might hit upon some better plan than to let the majority rule. The truth is, that the wise, the fair-minded, the honest and righteous, if we could only find them, ought to steer the Ship of State. Why should not the wise and the virtuous, the educated and the public-spirited have more weight and more votes than the selfish and the ignorant?' Why should not the man also who has property at stake, as well as his life, have more votes than the tramp who has not, perhaps, learned the language of our Country?

Many persons are saying such things as these in America. They think that a considerable number of the voters are too ignorant to be allowed to vote at all. They say that we have made a serious mistake in allowing the majority to rule. They believe that the power ought to be in the hands of such men as themselves, graduates of high-schools and colleges, owners of property, officers and members of churches. They imagine that the Country would be far better governed if a minority ruled. In some States in the Union it has been arranged so that the actual majority does not rule.

The truth is, that the world has had a very long experience with all sorts of methods to keep the majority from ruling. In our own Country we began by requiring that a citizen should have a certain amount of property, and, in Massachusetts, that he should be a member of the church. Such rules have held in England, where, till lately, the minority have governed the country. In the German city of Berlin, the owners of property have more votes than the poorer people.

It is curious to find that the better educated and well-to-do people, when they have had the whole power, have not succeeded very well in governing. They have voted for themselves and made laws for their own interests. They have not even agreed among themselves, but have often had bitter quarrels and sometimes civil war. To own property does not necessarily make men just or wise. To be educated does not make them always fair-minded, or friendly or patriotic. On the contrary, poor men, and even unlearned men, may be quite honest, and hearty patriots besides. Moreover, if ever the need comes to fight for one's Country, the poorest and most ignorant are called on to offer their lives. Is it fair, then, that they shall have no voice in deciding whether or not there ought to be a war? Is it fair that they shall not say whether they approve the laws under which they must live?

Let us suppose, however, that we are going to shut out a part of the people from voting. Who have the right to shut out the others? Have the rich a right to shut out the poor? Have the educated the right to shut out the unlearned? Have the good the right to put a brand on those whom they think to be bad? How can anyone tell in advance who is good and who is bad?

Thus it seems to be impossible to lay down any other rule than the one which we have made in America, namely, that the majority of *all* the people shall govern. Indeed, all the civilized nations in the world are marching along towards the same rule which we have established. This is not because the rule of the majority is always perfectly fair, but because we do not know any other plan that is so nearly fair. It will often happen that the minority, whom the majority has voted down, will not and cannot be contented. But this is not so bad as it was when the minority ruled and the majority were discontented, especially when they could not do anything to right their wrongs. It will doubtless sometimes happen that the majority will vote to do wrong things and will tax the others to pay for them, or will even compel the whole nation to do a wrong. But bad as this is, it is not so bad as when the minority of the nation do wrong continually and prevent the majority from setting the wrong right. Thus many a wicked war has been brought on in times past by only the few who have required all the others to pay and to fight.

We come now to what may be called the "safety-valve" of our American institutions. If the majority ever do wrong, if they are mistaken, or prejudiced, or unjust, *as long as all the people are free*, the few who are voted down to-day can persuade the others and get the majority themselves to-morrow. The majority will never stay on the wrong side very long.

There is a deep principle of justice underneath our American motto of Majority Rule. It is the principle of the Golden Rule. The idea is that when we are voted down we will behave as we would wish the others to behave when our turn comes and we vote them down. It is with men in carrying on the government as it is with the boys on the play-ground. It often happens that the boys cannot agree. There will be boys who, when they cannot have their own way, stop playing and go home. We call it mean and selfish in the boys to spoil the play for all, merely because they do not happen to be suited. We like the boys who give up their own way and play the game out and wait till some other day when their turn will come.

Certain hard questions however remain, and I propose in another chapter to show what rights the minority has and what the majority ought to do in order to protect these rights.

QUESTIONS

What is the *majority*? When have all the people ever voted *one* way? How do you account for the fact that people so often disagree? Is this a good or a bad thing, in the long run?

What ways can you think of for settling differences of opinion? What is our American motto? What did the Civil War teach us?

What faults can you see in the working of majority rule?
Would you believe in it if you lived in Mexico? What
wrong or foolish things can you recall that majorities
have voted to do? About what sort of things are
majorities very likely to be in the wrong?

What sort of people ought really to govern? Can you
think of any plausible reasons for letting the richer
people or the educated have more votes than the poor
and the ignorant? Do you think that the graduates of
the high-schools would give us a better government
than we have now?

Show where the world has tried the experiment of minority rule. How has the experiment worked?

What reasons can you give for letting all the people
vote? Can you think of any set of people who are
good or wise enough to have the right to shut out
their fellows from voting?

Why, on the whole, do we believe in the majority rule?
Can you think of any other better plan?

What is a safety-valve? What is the safety-valve of our
American institutions? What chance has a discontented minority always in America?

What has the Golden Rule to do with our idea of the
majority? Give an illustration.

Burdens become light when cheerfully borne.—*Ovid.*

You have not fulfilled every duty unless you have fulfilled that of being cheerful and pleasant.—*Buxton.*

If I can put one touch of a rosy sunset into the life of
any man or woman, I shall feel that I have worked with
God.—*G. Macdonald.*

No man has come to true greatness who has not felt in
some degree that his life belongs to his race, and that
what God gives him He gives him for mankind.—*Brooks.*

THE AMERICAN PATRIOT

MINORITIES AND THEIR RIGHTS

We have agreed when people differ about the conduct of their government, that the fairest rule, on the whole, is to do what the larger number, or the majority, prefer. But we have had to admit that this favorite American way has great dangers. The truth is, that a number of men may be as tyrannical as any king or despot. A majority may be wilful, unjust, cruel and oppressive. There are communities in the United States where the minority are not even allowed to express their opinions. Ignorance is always intolerant of opposition.

In framing a government there must therefore be fair provision made for safeguarding the minority. This is really for the good of the majority also, for we have already seen that the majority is extremely apt to make mistakes and to get upon the wrong side. All new ideas for better government, all reforms of old abuses, are likely to originate with a few persons. The majority do not care for the new ideas; they very likely distrust them. It is indeed through the growth of minorities to become majorities that everything good is brought about. Thus in the old days before the Civil War it was at first only a minority of people who resisted the spread of slavery into our new States. They were unsuccessful for many years. At last, however, the great Republican party grew out of this "Free Soil" minority, and swept the country with their votes. Every intelligent person is now glad that they succeeded. It has proved to be good for the whole country—for the South as well as for the North—that the anti-slavery minority was not suppressed, as many once desired.

What has happened once, is always likely in some new form to happen again. New questions are forever coming up. The old successful majority wakes up to see a new minority threatening to supplant it and turn it out. Our laws therefore are intended to give all needful freedom for the minority of to-day to become the majority to-morrow.

One way in which we secure fair play for the minority is by the frequency of our elections. It is possible that in some cases we have elections too often. But this is better for our liberties than it would be to make the elections very infrequent — once in eight or ten years, for instance. As it is now, the people in power have to defend their position by good behavior, or they will be turned out. Besides, the ideas which the minority stand for are published abroad at every election; they are discussed; they are criticised and defended and brought into more clearness. The people are educated by having to think about them and understand them.

The minority are also given fair play in our country by the fact that we are divided into so many political bodies. The minority is not obliged to wait till it can become the majority of all the people of the United States; but it may win its way in one State at a time; or, even when it is yet the smaller number in the State, it may have a majority in some of the towns or cities. Its leaders have thus a chance to try their hand at actual government, and often to apply their principles and to give an object lesson of how they will work. Thus the Prohibition principle is on trial before the country to-day. It controls a minority in the Nation. But it has certain States in which it is at work showing the American people whether or not it is desirable to be applied everywhere.

It is evident that the minority ought to enjoy perfect freedom of speech and of the press. Suppose, as in Russia and indeed in Germany, the people with the new ideas were liable to arrest whenever they spoke in public. Suppose the laws did not protect their newspapers, but as in the case of the brave Lovejoy in Illinois, a mob was allowed to destroy the printing office and kill the editor. Or suppose the majority in Congress were unwilling to hear the petitions of the unpopular minority, as was the fact when John Quincy Adams, "the old man eloquent" from Massachusetts, vindicated the sacred right of petition; whenever the minority are not suffered to utter their thoughts, the majority strike at the liberties of all the people.

Yes, some one says, but what if the minority are foolish and wrong? The truth is, it is bad enough to be foolish and wrong and on the unpopular side, without being muzzled also. Indeed, there is no help so great to rescue men from their folly as to require them to publish and explain it and let the daylight in upon it.

Another protection which we give to the minority is by our *veto* system. The Mayor, or the Governor, or the President is supposed to represent the whole body of his citizens. He does not belong to the majority merely, who have elected him, but when chosen he is in office for the interests of all. If therefore the majority seem to him to have passed an act hurtful to the people, he is required not to sign the bill and so to let it become law, but to return it to the Council or Legislature or Congress that passed it, with his objections. The rule is then, that if it is passed again over his veto, it must have not merely a majority of votes as before, but as large a number as two thirds of the votes.

This is not the only case when the rule is to require more than a majority of the votes. For instance, if the majority wish to alter the Constitution of the State or the Nation, and, for example, to introduce into it a clause prohibiting the liquor traffic, this change cannot be made by a mere majority. Such rules illustrate the extreme desire of those who framed our institutions to give the minority all possible protection.

The Constitution itself is a resource against the abuse of the minority. Let a careless majority pass an injurious law threatening the liberties or the property of any class of the people, and the courts are open to determine whether the law is in line with the Constitution, and if not, to set it aside. The courts have repeatedly disapproved such laws in the interest of justice to the minority.

It ought to be noted in passing that almost everywhere there has been a breaking down of the majority rule in favor of a plurality. Thus when an election is held for Mayor or for President, the winning candidate is not the one who gets the majority of all the votes, but the one who gets more than any one else. By this custom we have actually made it possible for a clear minority of the people of the United States to control the Executive branch of our government. As a matter of fact, when Mr. Lincoln was elected the first time, a majority of the citizens of the Republic were opposed to the ideas for which he stood. In a city, likewise, it may be possible for a party with only one third of the votes to get complete control of the city. This change to the plurality rule carries very grave objections and may sometimes actually mean the frustration of the will of the majority.

In spite of all our provision for the minority, bad abuses are still possible. Suppose in the State of Vermont a third of the people are Democrats and the rest are Republicans. It may happen for years that the Democrats of the State are never represented in Congress, and hardly at all in the Legislature. Here is taxation without representation! Suppose that a quarter of the people of a city wish unpartisan administration. It may be with our present system that this minority never can elect an

Alderman. In other words, on a Board of sixteen men, where they would be entitled honestly to four places, they have no place. Here is a defeat of the purpose of representative government. In a true representative body each party of citizens surely ought to have its fair proportionate share of votes. There is accordingly a movement on foot to correct this evil by what is called Proportional Representation. The idea appeals to the sense of fair play in the American people. When it is carried into effect, the majority will still rule, that is, will hold the executive reins, and will pass the laws, but each reasonable minority will have a voice in making the laws, and will have its vote counted whether for or against the proposed law.

Is it not possible, some one may still ask, even in the United States, that the majority will carry laws which would compel the minority to do what they think to be wrong? The old law which required free men to restore slaves to their masters was such a law. The Sunday laws in some States seem to be an oppression to the Seventh Day Baptists or to the Jews. The fact is, it is hard to live in human society and yet be independent and conscientious, and not sometimes have to take the unpopular side. Sometimes duty requires us merely to speak and to vote with the few. Sometimes one must bear ridicule and even abuse. It may be that petty injustice will be done. But it is very rare that duty bids the minority to resist the action of the laws except by agitation and argument. The good and the true is always stronger than the bad or the false. It only needs plenty of light and it will win the many to its side.

Questions

Do you know of any instances in which the majority has been tyrannical? Why cannot new ideas generally be popular? Why ought we to thank the pioneers who bring us new political ideas?

Give illustrations of such new ideas that began as unpopular and finally won over the multitudes.

How does it help the minority to allow frequent elections? What objection, if any, do you see to this custom?

What is a strongly "centralized" government? Give an instance of such a government. What advantages have minorities in our country because we are not centralized?

How far do you believe in perfect liberty of speech? Would you let " anarchists " publish what they thought? Give reason for your answer. What safeguard have we against all foolish ideas?

What is the *veto* power? Show how it works in some particular case. How does it tend to protect a minority? To whom does the Governor or the President belong?

Can you give instances where a two-thirds vote is required? Why would not this be a good rule always? Do you think it would be right for a majority of the people to enter upon a war against the protest of a large minority of the people?

How may oppressive laws often be set aside?

What objections do you see to the plurality system? What reasons are there in its favor?

What is Proportional Representation? Show the need and the fairness of it.

What ought a minority to do if they are oppressed or bidden to obey unjust laws? Would it ever be right in a free country to take up arms against the laws?

THE AMERICAN PATRIOT

CHAPTER 12

TRUSTING THE PEOPLE

We have seen that it is our American way to let the people rule. This splendid experiment which we are working out in this country springs from a deep principle which deserves careful attention. It is the principle of trust. In other words we in America believe in trusting one another, in trusting our neighbors, in trusting the people who live on the other side of the continent, in trusting the men in the other political party and not our own party alone, in trusting even the thousands of immigrants who come over here from Russia, Italy and Hungary.

This is rather a new idea in the world. Not all Americans have yet caught its meaning. The common habit of mankind has been to treat each other with suspicion or fear. There is a great deal of suspicion everywhere. Men who deem themselves quite fit for any office often seem to doubt whether their neighbors have any common sense. Men often distrust the people in the opposite party, and fear, if they get into power, that they will ruin the country. There are many good people who are extremely shy of all "foreigners." They imagine that certain classes of immigrants are hostile to our government. They fear that men come to plot against our institutions, our liberties, our public schools. All these fears and suspicions survive from the wild times when men thought that most other men, especially men of another tribe or

language, hated them.   These suspicions come over here
still from the armed camps in which the governments of
Europe continue to keep their people ready for war.   We
certainly have to face the fact that these fears and suspicions have deep and long roots and are not easily cast
out of men's minds.   Nevertheless the foundation of our
American system of government is in the new idea of
trusting one another.

Let us see how much this new idea means, and be sure
that it is really practicable to trust men.   Some years ago
the famous missionary explorer, David Livingstone, made
his way, unattended by a single white companion, across
the continent of Africa.   He had to pass through numerous savage tribes who could easily have robbed and
killed him.   Most men would have said in advance that
he could never accomplish his undertaking.   But his ar-
mor was in his fearlessness and trust.   He treated the
blacks as men and friends, and he expected friendly treatment in return.   To expect the best of men is to help them
to give their best.   If Livingstone, on the contrary, had
shown any fear or suspicion he would have called out the
suspicion and hate of the savages and he would have un-
doubtedly been killed immediately.   So marvelously the
new idea of trust works even among wild men !

We all know the same fact in thousands of schools.
Let the teacher expect mischief, let him show suspicion
to his scholars, let him, worse yet, imagine that his boys
take him for their natural enemy and he will invariably
have trouble with that school.   He will show the boys
by his suspicion that he does not know human nature.
But let the teacher assume from the start that he and the
boys are friends, let him look for honor and fairness in
the school, let him expect their best of his scholars, in
short let him trust them and he will get what he expects.
True, they will be boys still, they will not be rid of all
their faults at once.   But the habit of trust will prove the
key to the best possible success with the school.

Now we in America believe in the working of the
same rule of trust, without which our government simply
cannot go on. We assume that the average citizen means
to be fair and just. We hold that, much as he wants his
own interests to flourish, he does not intend to trample
on our interests. We assume, even when he votes
against us, that he does not mean to wrong us if he gets
the power. If he is at the West and we are at the East
we assume that he loves the common country and re-
gards the common flag. If he is a rich man and we are
poor, we are slow to suspect that he would oppress us.
If he is a Socialist and we think that he is mistaken, we
do not believe that the Socialists propose to take away
any real rights which we possess. If he is fresh from
Bohemia we choose to assume that he will swing into
line and help support our American institutions. If he is
a Catholic and we are Protestants, we expect him to be
a patriot in America. Some one will shake his head and
say that these are bold assumptions. I reply that only so
far as we proceed on these assumptions and actually trust
one another, has our government any strength. Wherever on the contrary you find enmity, distrust, the lively
expectation of mischief and conspiracy, you find popular
government endangered.

The story of the Civil War illustrates this law. The
Civil War was bred of suspicion and partisan and sectional distrust. Lincoln trusted the people that they would
do the fair thing. If the party leaders, and especially
those in the South, had trusted the people as Lincoln did,
it is safe to affirm that the war could not have taken
place. The method of trust, congenial with our institutions, would have found another way to get rid of slavery.

I know what some will answer. They see in our government only a sort of rude conflict of competing and
hostile interests, as when the billiard ball by repeated
blows, each in a different direction, at last comes to a
stop. So they say that which is done by the conflict of

votes is the resultant of the diverse energies of men and parties who suspect one another as enemies. There is a show of truth in this picture. But the deeper truth is that in all our conflicts we are always learning better to trust each other. We have found out repeatedly that there are good and fair men in the other party. When they have got into power they have not wrecked the ship. Whenever we have appealed to their sense of justice they have been willing to meet us. In fact they are human like ourselves. We do our best when others expect our best of us. So do the men of the opposite party.

What shall we say, however, to this square objection against trusting the people? It is urged that they are not yet just or intelligent enough to be trusted. As a matter of fact, they are full of all kinds of prejudice. They go crazy with wild theories about money and other difficult subjects. They are easily led by demagogues. It may indeed be necessary to let them vote, but how can one help fearing the people, being such as they are, with millions of the ignorant and uncivilized?

We trust the people precisely as we trust the boys in the school-room, or as Livingstone trusted the wild men. We do not trust them blindly, but intelligently. We do not hold that they will always do wisely or that they will immediately do what they see is right. We merely insist that there are two distinct ways of treating them. One is to treat them on the side of their ignorance, and so to fear and suspect whatever they do. This is the old-world method through which the people were not regarded as fit to do anything except obey their masters. The other method is always to treat the people on the side of their manhood. This is to trust them, to take their advice, to give them responsibility, to respect their humanity, to appeal ever to their common sense and their conscience, to hope even if they fail to-day that they will do better to-morrow.

Let us see, however, whom else we should trust, if we

give up trusting the people. Shall we trust some one man? Or, shall we trust the men who own property? Shall we trust the educated men? Shall we trust the ministers of religion? The world has tried a good many experiments of all sorts and has met with constant disappointments. It does not make men trustworthy to give them property or education, or a long creed. The only experiment in trusting men that has ever worked has been on the ground, not of their property or their learning or their professions of religion, but on the simple ground of their manhood. A poor man, as far as his manhood goes, is just as trustworthy as a rich man. An unlettered man is as worthy of trust as a scholar, upon the sole ground which trust touches.

Moreover, it is not good for men to be trusted with other people's business, such as they can do for themselves. It is good to share in the business of the world. It is well to specialize certain men to do certain things, like inventing machinery, which they can do better than the rest of us. But suppose men bring to any one man, or to a few men, the decision of their own common affairs, suppose they leave to umpires the responsibility for using their time and spending their money, suppose they let others decide what trade they shall take and when they ought to marry—all this shifting of responsibility is bad at both ends—for the men who get rid of their own affairs and for the men who allow themselves to meddle with others' business. Neither does it matter how wise the meddlers are. If, therefore, we could find a hundred wise men to-morrow into whose hands we could put the whole political business of the American people, and who would not make any mistakes or spend one extravagant dollar, but who should tell us all precisely what to do, without the trouble of depositing a vote or ever entertaining a puzzling question, we would choose to go on as we do now, blundering all the time, but learning always better how to trust one another.

The truth is that to trust men to manage their own affairs is an education of their manhood. Trust a man in state-prison and you help to make a man of him. Trust the people, load responsibility upon them, appeal often to their patriotism and you civilize them. We in America are not merely seeking an honest and economical administration. We are seeking a nation of men who know what honesty and economy are.

Certain qualifications need, however, to be made. If we say that we trust the people we mean that we trust them when they are fully informed. The people, indeed, often disappoint their friends because they do not yet know the subject or the question upon which they vote. We must therefore give them plenty of time and information. Suppose we ask the people to vote on Proportional Representation. They will say *Yes* when they understand the issue, but meantime we must be patient with them.

Again, we can trust the people on simple questions, and especially whenever they can see a plain issue of right or wrong. The people thus thought out the issue of slavery quite rapidly, quite as fast as the rich men or the educated class, or the ministers of religion. But the people cannot be fairly asked to thresh out difficult problems, such as currency and banking. This is not because they are unworthy of trust, but because there are many subjects that need the wisdom and experience of experts. Thus the people may decide whether they wish to spend their money for a new State House or City Hall, but they ought not to pass upon the proposed plans of the new building.

It is here that our government becomes representative. The people, who are trusted in large and general questions, themselves trust their best aud most valued men (such is the theory, badly as it is as yet applied) to take up the public business in detail. The people commonly pay for the time of their representatives so as to have the benefit of their best service. They practically say to their representatives : Do your very best in our behalf. Is it not a shame that their representatives so often fail to hear or heed their commission?

QUESTIONS

What great principle is at the root of our government in America ?

What class of people, if any, ought not to be trusted? How does it work when men distrust one another?

Give instances to show what "trusting people" ac-accomplishes.

Do you think that the average citizen means to do justly by others? Do you think that our immigrants love the flag? What did they do in the Civil War ? What caused the Civil War ? Show what the habit of distrust had to do with it.

What was President Lincoln's method of treating men ?

How far can we trust ignorant citizens?

Is there any class of men who can altogether be trusted not to make any mistakes ?

How does trusting the people educate them ? What else do we want to effect by our government besides economy or efficiency ?

What must the people have in order to be trusted?

What sort of questions are most suited for decision by the whole people ? Give instances. What arrangement do we make to settle difficult questions ?

What single demand do we make upon our representatives?

Do you know what the "referendum" is ? What do you think of it ?

THE AMERICAN PATRIOT

CHAPTER 13

PUBLIC OPINION

The most mighty forces in the world are invisible. Gravitation and electricity are such forces. So in human affairs and in the government of nations the most active and efficient forces work out of sight. Such a force is what we have come to call public opinion. It is hard even to tell precisely what it is. We can explain it best by illustration. Thus it is the public opinion of a crowd of school boys that it is mean business to tell tales to the master. There is no law against a tell-tale. Indeed there are cases when it might be the duty of an honorable boy to try to prevent some disgraceful deed by exposing it. Nevertheless public opinion was strong against such a cause.

So likewise it was the public opinion in the American Colonies before the Revolution that the British Parliament was unjust in taxing America. Perhaps only a few people could have told why it was unjust to tax the Colonies which the the British government protected. There were doubtless honest tories in the Colonies, like Hutchinson of Massachusetts, who saw the British side of the question. Nevertheless, when somehow the idea flashed into the minds of a great many people that they were suffering an injustice, this made a different opinion. In general we may say that whatever people are feeling and thinking together, whatver they largely agree about, this public opinion. It is as if the minds and hearts of the people made a great stream running one way. Or, it is as if they were all magnetized, so as to point together in the same direction. When, therefore, the people are pretty evenly divided on any subject, or before they have made up their minds, we do not call this state of confusion or division public opinion. The stream may have eddies in its course, but in order to make good public opinion, the bulk of its volume must run decidedly one way.

It is worth noticing also that there is a sort of public opinion that belongs to every set or group or community by itself. Men arrange themselves like the variously colored strata of sand on a hill-side. There is a sort of public opinion of the lawyers and of the labor unions. There was a different public opinion in South Carolina in 1860 from that which was held in Vermont. The real public opinion, however, is that which sways the great mass of the people. It affects rich and poor, the better educated and the less educated, as, for instance, in the great wave of the public will of the people of the North to save the nation after Fort Sumter had been fired upon.

It is easy now to see what public opinion does. You find it at work in quite barbarous states. It limits the power of despots. They risk their thrones whenever they break over the lines of the established customs of their people. It is public opinion that make revolutions possible in Asia, as in Europe. Public opinion is stronger than armies, for the armies will not·fight against the cause which all men have at heart. Let public opinion in Germany grow in favor of peace, let the great masses of working people feel what they begin to feel now, that the interest of all the workers of the world are one, and no Emperor William could command a regiment to fight against the general opinion of the people.

Public opinion is deeper and stronger than laws and · institutions. If the laws do not express what the people really believe, if the laws require one thing and public opinion allows the opposite, no law can be long enforced. Thus the temperance laws depend everywhere upon public opinion. Even when the public vote these laws, if they do not honestly believe in them, the laws become a dead letter. On the other hand if any community had established a public opinion in favor of temperance, if it was a disgrace in that community to use the alcoholic beverages, if men there had learned better ways of spending their evenings than to frequent drinking saloons, in the presence of such a public opinion there would scarcely be the need of any temperance laws.

So with the institutions of government. There are so-called republics in South America which are not true republics. This is for the want of enlightened public opinion, on which all our liberties rest. The fear of the fathers of our nation was that some successful politician or general might usurp the government and destroy our freedom. They feared what the Napoleon' did in France. But the Napoleons could not have seized France if public opinion had not permitted them. Neither could any one ever seize the power in the United States unless the people were willing. If our fathers had reason for distrust it was because they could not quite trust our people.

Public opinion always seems to be shifting in its direction and its weight. It is liable to change its vote from one course to the opposite. Thus public opinion was at one time bitterly against any agitation of the subject of slavery; whereas now every one is agreed that slavery was a national misfortune. So public opinion was once everywhere in favor of the use of wine and beer; now there are millions of men and women who think wine and beer are as bad as poisons. This fickleness of public opinion is not altogether discouraging. Often it merely shows that the people have not yet thought about the subject and made up their minds. The same force of public opinion which protects a bad habit, when once changed to the other side, will preserve the new principle. It is safe to say that the nation will never change its mind back again to take up slavery. Neither will the nation go back to monarchy. Show the people that any practice like dueling is barbarous, and public opinion, which is fickle about new and untried things, does not change back again to that practice. The good habits, customs and principles once learned come to stay. Indeed public opinion may be likened to the growth of a tree. At the tips of the twigs, where the new life is growing, you can easily check or alter the movement of growth. But as soon as the wood has had time to grow hard, and especially in the firm trunk of the tree, you can not easily alter the direction.

The method of the working of public opinion in old times was mainly through what people said. The voice carried the current thought. One man told his neighbor; groups of neighbors talked together. Messengers galloped from one place to another. Orators addressed the people like Demosthenes at Athens. This was largely the case once in America. Now, at last, books and newspapers also add to the force of the popular current and give it direction. Cheap pictures make the unpopular thing ridiculous. The words of the orator are published for millions to read. Public opinion could never before move so fast and press with such weight. On the other hand there were never such masses of men to be stirred; there were never such dense layers of ignorance to be enlightened; there were never such difficult questions, such as money, the tariff, the wise government of great cities, on which public opinion has to be formed.

There is an evident danger that all this new machinery will be taken advantage of for the wrong ends. It is possible to stampede a crowd of minds for a little while, as hunters stampede a herd of buffaloes. Set the papers talking in any wild direction, send out pamphlets and speeches, and even a few designing or self-deluded demagogues may presently stir the minds of multitudes of voters, who will not thereafter be easily persuaded that they were led astray. In fact it seems at times as if the people were hypnotized by strange delusions. Nevertheless the sturdy faith of Abraham Lincoln holds good. "You can cheat some of the people all the time; and you can cheat all the people some of the time; but you never can cheat all of the people all of the time."

Moreover, what the mischievous or the ignorant can do on occasion in making and shaping public opinion, the wise and patriotic may do all the more forcibly. The good can and do write books and make speeches. They also can set the newspapers at work sowing the good seed broadcast. This has been illustrated a great many times. It is only a few years since all the offices of the government were made a means of bribery for the benefit of the party in power. Efficient and honest officers were turned out of their places whenever a new administration came in. There was no public opinion to hinder this gross injustice and abuse of the people's business. but a few disinterested men like George William Curtis, Carl Schurz and Dorman B. Eaton organized a little company of men who believed that the Civil Service ought to be for the benefit of the people of the United States. They wrote for the newspapers; they held meetings; they told their friends what ought to be done; they enlisted the best men in the great political parties in the endeavor to stop this kind of bribery; and now we find popular majorities, as in the city of Chicago, voting for Civil Service Reform. The truth is that the right thing. whenever the people see what it is, appeals to them as the thing to be done.

We get an idea here of what public opinion has to do with the running of our government. There is a Legislature or a city council who are tempted to do an unjust or extravagant thing. The few have usurped the real power and threaten to legislate for themselves or for some railroad which they are bribed to serve. Suppose now that the City or the State is filled with intelligent, independent and public-spirited citizens; suppose they call popular meetings at once; suppose all the papers show up the bad scheme; suppose numerous letters rain in upon the legislators protesting against the bad bill; is it not clear that public opinion is now the power behind the throne? No one will dare to face it when it is aroused.

Better still, suppose public opinion in favor of honest government has grown strong, suppose the people will not vote for selfish men, suppose they demand true, high-minded men who will serve the public without fear or favor, suppose thus a strong and enlightened public opinion is represented in the State House and in the City Hall—now you have in reality a "government of the people, by the people, and for the people."

QUESTIONS

What are the great forces of the world? What unseen forces are behind human affairs? Illustrate what public opinion is.

What sort of public opinion holds among lawyers or labor-unions? How was the public opinion of Vermont in 1860 different from that of South Carolina?

Give an instance of national public opinion; of international public opinion.

How does public opinion touch kings? How is it stronger than armies? How is it behind the laws? Which is the stronger, laws without public opinion, or public opinion without laws? Illustrate this.

Show how fickle public opinion often is. Why is not this discouraging?

How is public opinion made and guided? What danger can you see that bad men will make bad public opinion? Show how this has been done. What cure of this evil do you see? Give some instance of the making of good public opinion? How can public opinion stop abuses in government? How can it establish the highest kind of government? How can each one help in this?

THE AMERICAN PATRIOT

CHAPTER 14

HOW TO TREAT FOREIGNERS

Who are foreigners? Once the answer to this question meant almost all the people of the world. Each little Greek city stood by itself. Athens hardly had peaceful dealings with its neighbors, Thebes and Corinth, a few miles away. To Greeks all the rest of the world were barbarians. So with the Jews. Perhaps there were two or three millions of them, and all other people were Gentiles or "foreigners." Even the Samaritans, who spoke the same language and lived only a day's march from Jerusalem, were outsiders. After Europe called itself Christian, foreigners were everywhere thought to be "fair game" for the natives of each little kingdom to plunder, or cheat or insult.

We have taken a new idea about foreigners in America. In the first place we have bound forty States together, so that no citizen of one of them is a foreigner or outsider anywhere between the two oceans. Through thousands of miles, wherever an American travels, he is a citizen. Imperial Rome did this for part of its people, but we do it for all.

Moreover, most of our forefathers came from England; many came also from Ireland and Germany and Holland. We cannot think, therefore, of the lands from which our fathers came as foreign soil. No man in the world who speaks the English language is really a foreigner. No man who speaks German or Dutch or Norwegian, the language of our cousins, is a foreigner.

This is not all. We teach that foreigners are men like ourselves. Whereas, once it was thought that foreigners were inferior to natives, we say that all races of men are so many children of the one Father in Heaven. All are capable of improvement and civilization. But are not some peoples inferior to others? Yes. This may be, precisely as some native Americans are less strong and capable than others. This is a reason why the weaker or less able should have the more patience and sympathy shown them. It is not a reason why they should be despised and, much less, hated. So if any foreign people are really inferior, we do not propose for that reason to handicap them and make their lot worse.

The fact is, we do not much like to use the word "foreigner." A bit of familiar history will show us why. It is only a little while since we ourselves were strangers on this continent. We were all foreigners when we came over. What right have we, then, whose fathers happened to be on the ground a little earlier, to call other men just like ourselves foreigners who have arrived more recently? Or what sense is there in calling the people foreigners over the sea, who are the fathers and mothers, and brothers and sisters of those who are our own fellow citizens?

All this was so simple to the founders of our republic that they conceived the idea of making this land a sort of home of refuge and a land of promise for the oppressed people of the world. Our national doors were thrown open. Here was plenty of land, and, as they thought, work enough for all willing hands. No nation had ever been so largely hospitable. The new comers were soon made citizens with equal rights. Thousands of these new comers fought side by side with the native born in the Civil War. Truly the word "foreign" is becoming outgrown in America.

A grave question, however, faces the American people just now. Shall they go on treating all comers with this hearty welcome? There are new languages and more distant natives coming to our shores. Italians, Poles, Russian Jews, Armenians are appearing in thousands. Great capitalists encourage their coming, so as to have plenty of cheap labor at hand. Steamship companies advertise to the millions to come to America, and make great profits out of very cheap fares. Once a few emigrants came at a time in little sailing vessels. Once they had saved money to buy a farm. Now a single ship may bring a thousand, They come often with hardly more than the clothing they wear. Sometimes it is suspected that their own government helps to pay the passage money in order to get rid of men and women who are too ignorant to earn an honest living at home. Moreover, over the western sea, lies China with its hundreds of millions of people, industrious and temperate, but very poor, and willing to live upon what an American workman would waste. Meantime in our great cities are too many already who cannot get work enough to keep them from the danger line of cold and hunger. Thus the conditions of life in our great Republic have changed. Shall we still keep our doors wide open to the world and bid all men welcome? Or must we begin to put up barriers as though other people were strangers?

One point remains perfectly clear. It was always well to treat strangers as men, as we would wish to be treated. We must do the same still. It does not follow that we must let the governments of Europe and the great steamships send us more people than we can make happy or comfortable. If the table is full of guests it is not only unkind to those who are seated, but it is unkind to the new-comers to crowd them into the room. Let the latter wait a little till there is vacant space. It may even be desirable, and quite friendly on occasion, for the host to warn the traveling public that his house for the present is full and that accommodations had better be sought elsewhere. So wi h the nation. If we have half a million or more people who cannot get continuous work, that is, who have not found their proper place in our American life, it cannot be true national hospitality to encourage others to come to us till we have taken good care of those who are now here. On the contrary, we owe it to the poor people of Italy and Russia to try in some way to inform them of our situation. This is not treating them as " foreigners," but as men like ourselves.

Moreover it does not seem to be clear that we in America are helping the people who are left at home in the old countries by taking their emigrants. Do we relieve Ireland or Germany or Poland by providing homes for their working people ? No. The people who stay behind in these countries go on suffering, sometimes from misrule, sometimes from bearing the burden of great armies and heavy taxes, and sometimes from actual oppression.

Perhaps the greatest service that America has done for suffering nations has been in giving an object lesson of how a people may be happy and strong, without kings and noblemen to rule it, without big armies and navies, whose States are not separated by Custom-houses, who are free to travel and trade everywhere on equal terms, who have learned to treat each other as neighbors. If we take emigrants faster than we can make them happy and find places for them at our table, we shall cease to be so good an object lesson of "a government of the people, by the people, and for the people." It is time now for other nations to try to work out our experiment for the sake of their own people. It may do no harm if some of the emigrants stay at home and urge their governments to make their own national life happier. We do not want a world in which there shall be one or two great powerful republics, and all the rest of the nations shall be under the yoke of soldiers and emperors. We want a world in which all the nations shall be finally as free and as happy as we have been.

This brings us to another question, namely, how our government ought to treat other governments. The old way was to suspect, if not to hate, the governments across the border or over the sea. What was good for England, men thought, must be bad for France. What was bad for Europe must be good for America. Yes, men have often imagined it right to try to take advantage of the "foreign" government, to cripple its power and rob it of territory. This was because men were uncivilized. It was also because nations often claimed territory that did not rightfully belong to them. Thus, when kings of England fought to hold lands in France, it was not strange that the kings of France watched their chance to get their French lands back.

We are learning new ideas at last about other governments. One of these new ideas is that the safest thing in the world is to treat every other government with perfect justice. We in America wish nothing that really belongs to England or Russia. We propose to be quite honest. If we could get a slice of Canada by cheating or by force we would scorn to attempt it. To be just is better for a nation than to have a whole fleet of battleships. In fact it is the selfish and unjust government that needs to fight, as it is the thief or the rogue who has most reason to be afraid of his fellows.

We are learning also that it is safe and wise to treat other governments frankly, instead of being suspicious of them. Governments are made up of men, and they behave as men do. If any one shows fear and suspicion of his neighbor, if he carries pistols when he meets the other, if he has "a chip on his shoulder" and expects to be insulted, he tempts the other to carry pistols also and perhaps even to insult him. Whereas, if he is fearless as an honest man can afford to be, if he expects his neighbor to behave "like a gentleman," and therefore acts like a gentleman himself, this conduct goes a good way towards helping the other to behave likewise. This is human nature. So if the Government of the United States expects fair and friendly treatment of Great Britain, this helps the British Government to be friendly toward us.

We are learning also that it is not a good thing for America when Europe is in trouble. In fact when the people over the sea suffer and are poor, they cannot buy what America has to sell. But when the nations are all prosperous, trade is good here and there is a market for the products of our farms and shops.

The truth is that the nations of the world are growing to be a great commonwealth. We all really belong to each other. What is good for one, as a rule, is good for the rest. What hurts one hurts others, as in the human body each part or member is needful to the rest. It follows then that armies and war ships already begin to appear to all thoughtful persons as a terrible barbarism. They are as foolish between governments as it is foolish between neighbors to build stone walls, mount cannon and carry firearms. The time is coming when civilized people will settle questions between each other by some sort of International Court, as all reasonable men now settle the private differences over which their ancestors fought duels. Children will wonder that our generation should have been teaching the Golden Rule in the Sunday School while we were building wicked " commerce-destroyers " to sail the high seas. Nothing short of this reign of law and justice is the grand prophecy of civilization.

— : THE END : —

QUESTIONS.

What do you mean by a "foreigner?" What did Greeks and Hebrews once mean by " barbarians " and " Gentiles ?"

How large a number do we in America include as fellow-citizens? Did any nation ever do the like before? Do we call our cousins over the sea "foreigners?" When, if ever, is it well to draw the "foreign" line?

Are any people inferior to others? If so, how should the sronger treat the weaker?

Why do we not much like the word *foreigner?* Were our fathers ever "foreigners?" If so, when and how?

How did our land become a home for the oppressed? Have the new-comers ever failed to stand by the flag?

Is there now a new kind of emigration to America? Are we as able as ever to receive emigrants? Show how the conditions have changed.

What kind of treatment must we always show to strangers? Is it the part of kindness to let all the people who may wish, come to our shores? What ought we to do for the greatest good of the greatest number?

What is the greatest service that America has given to other nations? What ought other nations now to do for themselves? What is your idea of the happiest kind of world?

What was the old idea of treating neighboring governments? How did England once feel towards France? Why was this?

What is the safest conduct towards another nation? What sort of persons or people are most likely to get into a quarrel?

Show how frank and gentlemanly treatment works towards helping others to show the same.

Is it good or bad for us that other nations are prosperous? Give your reasons.

How are the people of the world truly related to each other? Ought there ever to be wars? Why is war a "barbarism?" How ought nations to settle their differences? Do you see any difficulty in this method?

What is the prophecy of civilization?

www.ingramcontent.com/pod-product-compliance
Lightning Source LLC
Chambersburg PA
CBHW031439270326
41930CB00007B/781

* 9 7 8 3 3 3 7 3 0 6 5 3 3 *